The Past Lives Workbook

BY: *Red Orchid Publishing*

MELANNY EVA HENSON

Table of Contents

For as long as we suppress the Goddess, we will continue to seek

Introduction

Thank you for trusting me to offer guidance with your past life journey. I would like to start with a little about myself and my philosophies before we begin. It is not necessary for you to believe everything that I believe, so I don't want my spiritual truths to come across as preachy or fixed tenets that you should adhere to if you want to engage in this process successfully, Instead, use any contrast between my instruction and your beliefs to gain a solid understanding of your own beliefs and practices. That process, (and not accepting every suggestion in this book) will result in the greatest growth in understanding yourself. It will build your confidence and ground you in future meditations because in addition to learning about the exploration of past lives, you are learning to trust yourself.

I will specifically mention Spirit, the spirit world, and Guides, but it isn't necessary for you to accept those concepts completely in order to benefit from past life exploration. Narrative is immensely powerful. The stories you tell yourself can be transformative. So even if you find yourself on the more pragmatic, agnostic spectrum of spiritual thought, try to relinquish yourself for a moment and dive into narrative. Give yourself permission to explore. You'll be amazed at what you uncover.

So with that, a bit more about me as your teacher before we get into the nuts and bolts of past life exploration. I am a mystic Christian witch. I grew up in Logan, Utah. I joined the LDS church when I was 15, and I was married in the Mormon temple a week before my 19th birthday. Over the next sixteen years, I earned an MFA in Creative Writing from *Iowa State*, and a Masters in Teaching from *Drake*. Graduate school brought an enormous shift for my life. I wanted to write about my church since it was my passion. But the more research I did about the history of the Mormon church, the more confused and disoriented I became. My feminism blossomed during this time as well. I distinctly remember reading essays by Mormon women discussing Mother in Heaven and using their priesthood power (even though we women were not supposed to). It was these essays that inspired me to make a dramatic change in my life and my spirituality.

This transition would prove wise because I would begin a journey that deepened my spiritual understanding and emphasized the value and importance of my life through using my God-given spiritual gifts. But this dramatic change would also be incredibly painful, as everything about my life changed completely. During this period, my mediumship abilities cracked wide open. I saw, heard and felt supernatural things that I did not understand at that time. I think trauma and loss sometimes pushes us towards Spirit when our brain chemistry is adaptable to such receptions. It was also during this time that I had my first profound experience with a past life connection. That experience would change the course of my life, for it was here that a deep belief in reincarnation was planted.

Another key shift occurred when I offered to read tarot for a friend I had made online. She called me, and as I was reading her cards, her deceased husband "showed up." I never see the spirits, but I have what is called, "clairaudience" and hear a distinct voice in my head. (It's quite similar to writing a story, but there's an energetic vibe that's recognizably different). Well, this was the first time this had happened in such an overt, undeniable way! I knew his first initial, how he died, what his personality was like, his hobbies, how he felt about things, etc. I felt like I had met him in person. When I hung up from that phone call, I knew something undeniably amazing was happening to me.

A couple days later, my cousin's wife, Shannon, posted about how much she missed her grandma and wished she could speak with her. I sent her a Facebook message and said I thought I could help. My theory proved correct. I could connect at will. And that was the beginning. Shortly after, I began charging for my services. Over the next six years, I would do mediumship readings regularly, I would found Red Orchid, and my life and spirituality would be forever altered.

Though I identify with pagan thought, Goddess worship, and feel quite comfortable with the label, "witch" I still identify as a Christian. This is unusual, I realize, and I often feel like I managed to alienate myself from everyone because of who I chose to be. I was often urged to "pick a side" by other spiritual people I admired. I felt a certain amount of pressure to relinquish myself to one walk over the other. But my Christian heart remains part of my essence. My witchy power is also a fundamental part of who I am (and is not, in my mind, anything evil or to be ashamed of). I love both my Father in Heaven and my Mother in Heaven (The Mormon term for Goddess). I am forever reverent and in awe of the power of Christ's narrative. I have felt the Holy Spirit enrapture me both in Christian churches and in my own private, pagan-centered meditations and rituals. Though at times I feel the tension of trying to ride the center of a dichotomy, I know my power grows because I am true to who I am.

So this sums up what a complex being your teacher is! I suppose the one advantage here is that no matter where you are on a spiritual spectrum, you should find my approach relatable in moments, since my faith encompasses a broad spectrum. I won't teach Christianity or Paganism directly during this course, but you should know that both of these paths influence my approach to this workbook.

Shall we begin?

A brief note about cards:

> You should use a tarot deck for use with this book. If you are experienced with cards, an oracle deck could also be used, though the reference guides will be more complicated to navigate. If you want to use the best resources available for this process, I recommend, <u>The Art History Tarot for Past Lives</u>, for which this workbook was created. You can purchase a copy at
> redorchidpublishing.com

You can book a private reading with me by sending a message to the *Red Orchid Publishing* Facebook page.

Happy Divining!

-Melanny

Before you Begin: Preparation, Ritual and Pre-Assessment

In preparation for the first day, we are going to discuss preparing your space, executing a protection ritual, and completing a pre-assessment. A pre-assessment is the initial activity for the course that you will use as a comparison point for the final assessment. In professional teaching, we always begin a learning unit by giving the students what we call a pre-assessment. It's a barometer to see how much the student already knows and perhaps to gauge their confidence level handling the material. Why? Because we can compare it to the final assessment and demonstrate that the student has learned something. Of course, spiritual practitioners don't have an administration to report to, so the pre and post-assessments are only for you, to help you reflect on how much you've grown over the course of the learning in this book.

A small note about the Dream Journal: There are journal pages at the back of this workbook for recording your dreams. Starting tomorrow morning, record every detail you can remember about your dreams. We will use this for the "Dreams spreads" section near the end of the course. You will need at least one dream for those spreads. Occasionally, I will run across someone who rarely ever dreams. If this is you, don't lose hope! Having started this course, your subconscious and spirit know you are seeking this information, and the chances are greater for receiving a dream during this time. It is for those students who rarely dream that I want to start the journal now: this will give the more sporadic dreamers a greater chance of capturing a dream for that coursework. In the case that you don't have any dreams over the next couple weeks, select a dream that you can recall with as much detail as possible.

SPACE

Is space really important? According to your teacher--yes! Geometric patterns forged through belongings, the presence of all the various molecules, and color dynamics within a space all facilitate energy: the arrangement of your home will attract and deflect certain types of energy. For that reason, I have some explicit instructions about your reading area for this course.

First is cleanliness. You should be working in a clutter-free, dirt-free space. Ideally, you are working in an environment that is visually pleasing and uplifting, but I understand that money restraints can often prevent us from reaching our lofty interior decor goals. If time constraints or simply the amount of work required makes it impossible to clean your home to your optimal self-pleasing level, let's settle for a corner of a room. Get this corner as beautiful as humanly possible. Remove all clutter, dirt, and debris. Decorate the space with beautiful items that uplift your spirit and calm your nerves. Small, table water fountains and natural stones are a good start, but anything that you find calming will work fine.

You will need a table to read cards on. It doesn't need to be a large table, but make sure there's enough space to spread out a deck of cards, and form a spread three rows high. Do not use this table for any other purpose other than your class during this time. This might seem silly, but try to remember all items hold energy. Half empty soda cans with evaporating carbonation, hats removed from tired and stressed heads, and that set of car keys with transitional vibrations can be disruptive to your space, and ultimately your connection to the cards. Learning divination, and particularly past life connection, is challenging enough without these kinds of energetic interruptions. If you have family members, you will need to start the communication now about not leaving anything on this table for the next few weeks. If your corner is in a high traffic area, you will probably end up reminding them. We are generally not accustomed to respecting space (and particularly tables) in this way.

RITUAL

I strongly recommend a grounding/centering or protection ritual before each session. Even if you don't believe you need spiritual protection, (and you're welcome to believe whatever you're comfortable with) a ritual can improve focus and concentration. Since we aren't doing a formal meditative regression, focus is acutely important. Over the years, I've learned how to both read and control the energy and space around me (and the more spiritually gifted you are, the more challenging this can be). Everyone's experience with Spirit is unique, but I can say with confidence that having a small, humble ritual before each session is a good idea. You may even want to spend 10-15 in with a past life regression meditation before beginning.

Which brings me to a rather intense topic very early on in this course: Is using cards spiritually dangerous? Some religious people think so. I don't think divination with cards is dangerous in that it invites evil into your life. Only your heart invites evil. But when you crack the door to the subconscious, when your imagination is let loose for a bit, like a caged dog it can run round and round and make you uncomfortable with its intensity. Sometimes cards can poke at your fears. Sometimes legitimate communication with the spirit world and with the Holy Spirit occurs. We always want those communications to be your guides, or beings of higher vibration, and not any other kind of spirit. One way to ensure that is with a brief clearing ritual. That's not to say that there are spirits communicating with you every time you use the cards. That hasn't been my experience. But you want to be prepared for those times, since you can't predict when they will happen. And you want to take the time to prevent negativity or lower vibrations before every session. In my opinion, it isn't wrong to seek counsel from Spirit through exercises such as cards. The spirit world wants to communicate with you and aid you on your journey, and angels and guides are ready and able to use these tools when you provide them. But you have to be deliberate in your method of connection to minimize spiritual interference and confusion. In my experience, a clearing ritual is potent and effective.

What your ritual is like should really be a reflection of you. I will share mine with you, but mostly as an example. If you feel stumped, you are welcome to use mine, but I encourage you to seek out your own voice for this ritual over time, for it will hold more power that way. If you are not an empath or if you don't have medium abilities, you may question whether you are communicating with Spirit at all during these sessions, and all that guide talk maybe sounds like nonsense to you. This is fine. Your ritual can reflect whatever makes you feel grounded, centered and at peace.

My ritual is entirely verbal and takes maybe 20 seconds to complete. I'll break each part down and explain why I use it and what it means for me personally. If you don't have a ritual, I encourage you to answer the prompts after each section to help you devise your own.

Father and Mother in Heaven,

This is the invocation. I am inviting the Most High Spirit into my heart and mind. The concept of Mother in Heaven was a common term in Mormonism, and a key tenet to major spiritual shifts in my life. I spent years on my knees praying daily to "Father in Heaven." We were forbidden to address Mother in Heaven in this same way. However, when I left Mormonism, I began incorporating Her into my daily invocation. Saying "Father in Heaven" offers the familiar and that sense of safety that I nurtured through years of practice. Saying "Mother in Heaven" honors my new truth and my personal power. I also feel a sense of peace and balance by acknowledging both male and female, without making a hierarchical choice of one over the other.

Questions to consider:

1. What memories do you have of feeling at peace spiritually, or feeling a strong connection to God?

_____

_____

_____

_____

_____

_____

2. What prayers or spiritual language from your childhood still feel good to you when you hear or say them?

_____

_____

_____

_____

3. What language reflects your perception or ideal image of God?

_____

_____

4. Reviewing your responses to the above, what invocation would feel the most right for you?

_____

_____

_____

Please cast a circle of white light around me,

When I was feeling particularly vulnerable, I did a lot of reading on white light. Diane Ahlquist has a wonderful book on this topic. Visualization is really important for me because I struggle with centering. So, when I say these words aloud, I imagine a large ball of white light encompassing me. I also imagine my Heavenly Parents there with me, ensuring that the light has been cast.

Please send Archangel Michael to remove any lower level vibrations from my presence,

This is technically a second invocation. I have spent some time helping people with hauntings, and I've found asking for Michael's help to be effective. He has a fast response rate and his customer service is excellent. ;) I don't ever engage in hauntings for entertainment reasons, (spirits can/might follow you home, and in my opinion, it's just not worth it) but I will get involved if someone needs help. I have always made connection and felt Michael's presence in these situations. Typically, more than one angel responds, the number corresponding to the severity of the situation. I'm always given a number by Michael to aid in visualization, which strengthens the angels' ability to do their task. So, I have a working relationship with Michael and feel comfortable and at peace including him in my ritual.

Question to consider:

5. Which angels, archetypes, or god/goddesses would you like to develop a closer relationship with?

_____

_____

_____

Please help me to see clearly for and on behalf of _____

Here, I am asking for help with focusing. It both grounds me and allows Holy Spirit to work more freely through me. If the reading is for me, I say "myself," or insert the name of the querent if I'm reading for someone else.

In the name of Jesus Christ, Amen.

This is the benediction. Because of some spiritual abuse in my past, there was a phase of my life in adolescence when the word and concept of Jesus had the exact opposite effect of forming a spiritual connection with The Divine. So if you find this particular language personally troubling, I completely understand. It is absolutely okay to move on and find new language that feels comfortable and peaceful for you. Though the specifics of what I believe have shifted dramatically through the years, I have ultimately left this inclusion at the end of my prayers. It is part of the prayer habits that I developed while forming a more personal relationship with God. I spent a great deal of time developing a channel to this specific language that raises my vibration. Although I firmly believe there are a myriad of ways to accomplish such a vibrational connection, and I don't believe the concept of Jesus is required for protection, at the end of the day, it's good to stick to language and experiences that you know have worked for you.

Question to consider:

    6. Which gods, angels or archetypes would you feel comfortable asking to bless your work?

       _____

       _____

       _____

    7. What language do you feel connects you to God (or the universe, or the earth)?

       _____

       _____

       _____

Protection/Clearing Ritual Worksheet

Now, you're going to take everything you've reflected upon in this section and create your own ritual. Create something beautiful, diverse, and powerful!

Primary Invocation:

_____

_____

Secondary Invocation(s) if any:

_____

_____

What I will visualize:

_____

_____

What I will specifically ask for:

_____

_____

Physical Gestures (include this if you think it would help. _Examples: sign of the cross, holding a crystal, etc)_:

_____

_____

Who (or What) I will ask to bless my work (Benediction/Closing):

_____

_____

Pre-Assessment

We are finally to the pre-assessment section! Get your cards and table ready, perform your clearing ritual, and let's get started. For this exercise, I want you to pull two cards, asking the question: *Who was I?* We are reaching in and asking for information about a past life. The most important past life, the one that most affects and influences you in this life, is the one that is most likely to come out on the first attempt.

What I call "pulling cards" is an acquired intuitive skill. You do get better at it with time. How do you do it? Well, first, you want to ensure that your draw is random, that the cards are shuffled, and you have no idea where one particular card may be. Stacking the deck for yourself is pointless as a spiritual practice. So it needs to be random.

Secondly, you need to hold the question in your mind. Ask the question aloud, and form it in your mind as though it is a little ball of thought, and imagine that ball in front of you, holding it suspended above the cards. Over time, my own intuitive pulling became visual--certain cards would take on visual properties that caused them to "stand out" while I looked over the deck. But that didn't develop until a few years in. Even though I am skilled at pulling cards, if my querent is present, I will always have them pull their own cards. The reason why is that your own intuitive process for a question about you is more potent than my own. Your intuition works best, even if you aren't feeling very connected or confident yet! Your intuition is superior in quality for you, even in the beginning learning stage. So go forward with confidence.

For this question, you're going to pull two cards, both with the question: *Who was I?*

Write the name of the card on each in the diagram below.

Card 1	**Card 2**

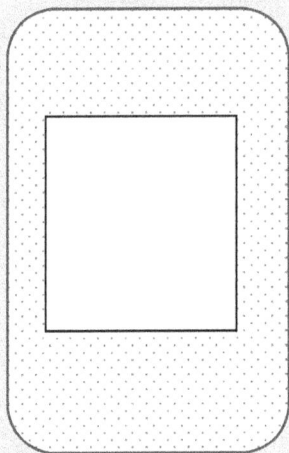 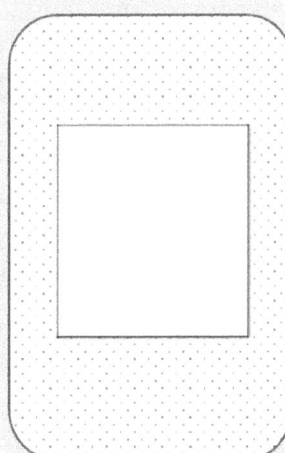

Next, we are going to do three types of readings: visual/spiritual, language, and deconstruction. There are many ways to read cards, so you're going to practice these three main ways in order to learn what type of card reader you are. Also, the type of reader you are can shift and change as you practice, so I don't want you to think of this as a fixed truth.

1. ## Visual/Spiritual

   For each of the cards, connect the images to your emotions. What do you feel when you look at this card? Forget, momentarily, what you know about the meaning of the cards or the words printed on them. Stay grounded in emotion/feelings, and what the image encourages you to feel, and not in ideas or language. Emotions are the language of Spirit, so you are most likely to make a connection and receive a message here, in this space.

   A.) What did you feel while looking at the image on Card 1?

   _____

   _____

   _____

   B.) What did you feel while looking at the image on Card 2?

   _____

   _____

   _____

After each reading, I want you to do a self-assessment to gauge your comfort level and success with this process.

   C.) On a scale of **1 to 10**, with **10** being "*I was overcome with emotion and nearly brought to tears*" and **1** being "*I must be Vulcan*," how emotional did you feel looking at the image on **Card 1**?

   1   2   3   4   5   6   7   8   9   10

D.) On a scale of **1 to 10**, with **10** being *"I was overcome with emotion and nearly brought to tears"* and **1** being *"I must be Vulcan,"* how emotional did you feel looking at the image on **Card 2**?

1   2   3   4   5   6   7   8   9   10

E.) On a scale of **1 to 10**, with **10** being *"I felt God/Goddess/Universe speaking directly to me through the card"* and **1** being *"This is only cardboard,"* how much of a spiritual connection did you feel gazing at the image on **Card 1**?

1   2   3   4   5   6   7   8   9   10

F.) On a scale of **1 to 10**, with **10** being *"I felt God/Goddess/Universe speaking directly to me through the card"* and **1** being *"This is only cardboard,"* how much of a spiritual connection did you feel gazing at the image on **Card 2**?

1   2   3   4   5   6   7   8   9   10

2. Language

Now you're going to focus on language in your response to the cards. You can examine what the language printed on the cards means outside of a tarot/oracle context, or you can focus on the language that is commonly associated with that card (this exercise will look vastly different depending on if you have experience with tarot or not).

A.) What are all the word/language associations you have with **Card 1**?

_____

_____

B.) What are all the word/language associations you have with **Card 2**?

_____

_____

I'd like you to build upon your existing knowledge of this language. Now, we are going to narrow the scope and shift away from every word association we might have, and instead focus on tarot/oracle interpretations. Get out the book that came with your deck, and find at least two more resources. These can be other books you have on hand, or websites. Research each of your cards and compare/contrast information between sources.

C.) What new language can you identify for **<u>Card 1</u>**?

_____

_____

D.) What new language can you identify for **<u>Card 2</u>**?

_____

_____

Next, let's make a comparison of all your language associations to your emotional response.

E.) When you compare your language associations to your emotional response for **<u>Card 1</u>**, how well do they align, if at all?

_____

_____

F.) When you compare your language associations to your emotional response for **Card 2**, how well do they align, if at all?

_____

_____

G.) On a scale of **1 to 10** with **10** being, "*My emotional response and language associations were completely in alignment*" to "*Neither card seemed to connect my emotional response to its intended meaning,*" how well do you feel your spiritual and intellectual response to these two cards aligned?

      1   2   3   4   5   6   7   8   9   10

3. Deconstruction and Application

Now that you have explored each card emotionally and intellectually, the third step is to apply that information to yourself in an interpretive way. Deconstruction is a term that means breaking down parts. Here, we break down the emotional and intellectual aspects of a card and then apply them in a personal and interpretive way.

Reflect over your responses to E and F on the previous page. With that information, we are going to apply it to our question: *Who was I?* This process involves evaluating the different aspects of the card, and then reconstructing those responses to apply to a potential identity (potential identity because that is the question we asked). Certain aspects of each card from the visual and language exercises will now come to the forefront, and certain aspects will now fade to the background or be eliminated entirely if they don't apply, if they contradict, or if they don't resonate with you.

Again, revisit your emotions during this process and rely on your intuition to tell you where the focus should go. Although I probably wouldn't deviate entirely from a card's intended energy, it's okay to reinterpret a card based on the image or where you feel your intuition is pulling you. What's important is that you understand to what extent you are deviating from the logical aspects of that card, so that you may do it with intention and clarity.

A.) Now, answer the question: *Who was I?*

Card 1:

_____

_____

Card 2:

_____

_____

B.) On a scale of **1 to 10**, with **10** being "I understood the deconstruction process perfectly and was able to apply this process with ease" and **1** being, "I feel I don't understand the deconstruction process," how comfortable were you with this last step?

1   2   3   4   5   6   7   8   9   10

C.) On a scale of **1 to 10** with **10** being, "I feel I was able to connect to and interpret these cards for myself" and **1** being, "I feel a total disconnection to the intuitive process," how connected to Spirit did you feel during the reading?

1   2   3   4   5   6   7   8   9   10

You have now completed the Pre-Assessment. We will do a similar exercise and reflection at the end of the workbook. I expect you will see tremendous growth and illuminating insights through these exercises as you work through them.

See you tomorrow for Day 1!

Days 1-3: Spiritual Essence Spreads

We are going to start the course focusing on your spiritual essence, those qualities that are unique to you and what you bring with you from your inception as a soul and your previous lifetime experiences. We all come from love and light. Some of us are more comfortable with shadows, some of us are called to shadow work, and some people are even intentionally placed as a polarizing force of opposition in the world. Some of us came to fight injustice and have stronger personalities that may seem difficult at times. But we all come from love and light, and it is part of everyone's essence.

One problem I anticipated while creating the spiritual essence spreads is that someone might pull a particularly dark or unpleasant card as a reflection of their essence. I don't think negative qualities should be part of your spiritual identity, and in fact, I think such a train of thought could be psychologically damaging and could reinforce spiritual blockages you are currently trying to work through. So, I'm providing a brief reference for using tarot to interpret spiritual essence. If you are using an oracle deck, find a similar tarot card that reflects the same base energy.

From here on out, we are skipping over the visual and language steps, and instead documenting the deconstruction and application phase of reading. If you are new to divination and would find it helpful to record the intermediary steps, two copies of blank forms are provided in the back of this book. Cut them out and make photo copies for as many as you think you will need.

Write the name of each card that you pull for the spread placement just like you did on the pre-assessment. You want to keep a record of which cards you pulled so you can look for repetition over the course of the work. I call repeating cards "the talkers," the cards that really seem to have a message and are trying to get your attention. You will notice that certain cards keep popping up. Pay attention! That's where divination is certainly happening.

Spiritual Essence Reference Guide

Major Arcana

0-The Fool	Angelic qualities; most likely a healer	11-Strength	An old soul with many lifetimes of hardship
1-The Magician	Resourcefulness; uncanny ability to manifest	12- The Hanged man	Unfinished business
2-The High Priestess	Metaphysical powers	13- Death	Eager to reincarnate
3-The Empress	Creativity	14- Temperance	Even-tempered; not easily given to extremes
4-The Emperor	Authoritative	15- The Devil	Connection to spirituality through sexuality
5-The Hierophant	Knows how to work the system	16- The Tower	Fearless; not afraid to start over if circumstances require that
6-The Lovers	Spiritual connection to sexuality	17- The Star	Faithful; rarely to never struggles to have faith for the future
7-The Chariot	Goal-focused	18- The Moon	Extremely psychic; career in mysticism, if chosen
8- Justice	A strong sense of justice; honest	19- The Sun	Optimistic and happy nature
9- The Hermit	Observant and meditates more easily than others	20- Judgment	Intuitively observant; strong connection to the higher self
10- Wheel of Fortune	Inspires change in others	21- The World	Naturally confident

Cups

Ace of Cups	Abundance of love	Eight of Cups	wanderlust
Two of Cups	Strong loyalty and commitment	Nine of Cups	Uncanny ability to get what you want
Three of Cups	social	Ten of Cups	Easily satisfied
Four of Cups	Lack of impulsiveness	Page of Cups	Willing to help others
Five of Cups	Passionate: loss hits you harder than most	Knight of Cups	Feels obligated to help others
Six of Cups	Family oriented	Queen of Cups	Loves strangers with ease
Seven of Cups	Dreamer	King of Cups	Benevolent love that others rely on

Swords

Ace of Swords	Writer; truth teller	**Eight of Swords**	Able to discern falsehood and illusion quicker than others
Two of Swords	Blind to others' negative qualities	**Nine of Swords**	Intense connection to spirituality through dreams with spiritual messages
Three of Swords	Broad emotional range; you feel emotions more intensely than others	**Ten of Swords**	Wanting and needing a fresh life to start over; desire to forget the past
Four of Swords	Acute compassion for the sick and suffering	**Page of Swords**	Natural planner
Five of Swords	Not afraid of confrontation	**Knight of Swords**	Warrior spirit
Six of Swords	Likes to travel	**Queen of Swords**	Articulate; defensive against injustice
Seven of Swords	Clever; able to anticipate problems and avoid them	**King of Swords**	Articulate; masterful writer

Wands

Ace of Wands	Exceedingly driven	**Eight of Wands**	natural technology skills
Two of Wands	A natural inclination to think about the future	**Nine of Wands**	Capable of seeing solutions most people don't
Three of Wands	Good karma from past lives	**Ten of Wands**	Strong multi-tasker
Four of Wands	Stable emotionally and physically	**Page of Wands**	Inspires others
Five of Wands	Competitive nature	**Knight of Wands**	Ambitious
Six of Wands	Blessed with many talents	**Queen of Wands**	Attractive personality, inspires envy
Seven of Wands	Intuitively knows how to deal with difficult people	**King of Wands**	Charismatic and natural leader

Pentacles

Ace of Pentacles	Natural abundance mentality	**Eight of Pentacles**	Likely to pursue higher education; lifetime student
Two of Pentacles	Natural performer; visual artist	**Nine of Pentacles**	Independent; comfortable living alone
Three of Pentacles	Team player	**Ten of Pentacles**	Talented at manifesting
Four of Pentacles	Good with money	**Page of Pentacles**	Animal lover and eco-conscious
Five of Pentacles	Minimalist tendencies; you don't need much; the opposite of materialistic	**Knight of Pentacles**	Homebody; likes routine
Six of Pentacles	Charitable	**Queen of Pentacles**	Nurturing and motherly
Seven of Pentacles	Hard worker; values hard work	**King of Pentacles**	Strong sense of responsibility to others

Day 1: Spiritual Essence Spread 1

1- Draw three cards that represent three different qualities of your spiritual essence for cards 1-3.
2- Draw one card that represents how all these qualities impact your life.
3- Draw one card that represents how these qualities might make you vulnerable

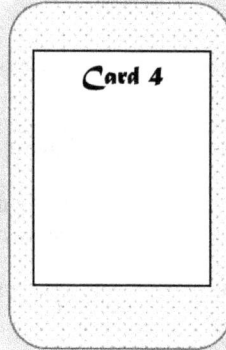

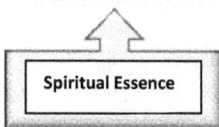

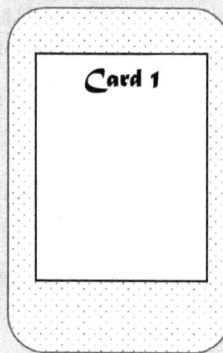

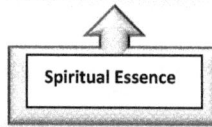

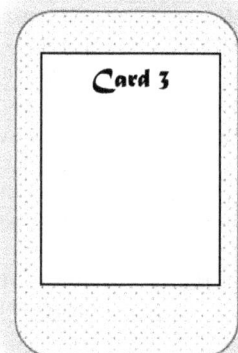

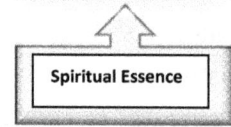

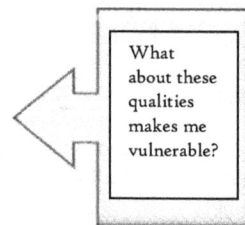

Card 4

What impact do these qualities have on this life?

Card 2

Card 1

Card 3

Spiritual Essence

Spiritual Essence

Spiritual Essence

Card 5

What about these qualities makes me vulnerable?

Note: All three cards probably won't connect to both 4 and 5, so follow interpretations that make the most sense, or where you feel pulled

Deconstruction/Application Day 1

1. Record your interpretations for each of the cards:

   Card 1:

   _____

   _____

   Card 2:

   _____

   _____

   Card 3:

   _____

   _____

   Card 4: *What impact do these qualities have?*

   _____

   _____

   Card 5: *What about these qualities makes me vulnerable?*

   _____

   _____

   What is the greatest insight you gained from this spread?

   _____

   _____

   _____

2. On a scale of **1 to 10**, with **10** being *"I definitely felt connected to my spiritual essence,"* and **1** being, *"I'm not sure I had any connection to my spiritual essence,"* how connected did you feel to this spread?

   1   2   3   4   5   6   7   8   9   10

Day 2: Spiritual Essence Spread 2

Pull one card for spiritual essence. Stay in the energy of that essence card and ask, how did this affect me in a past life? Then ask, how does this affect me now? Repeat twice more. Keep cards face down until the spread is complete.

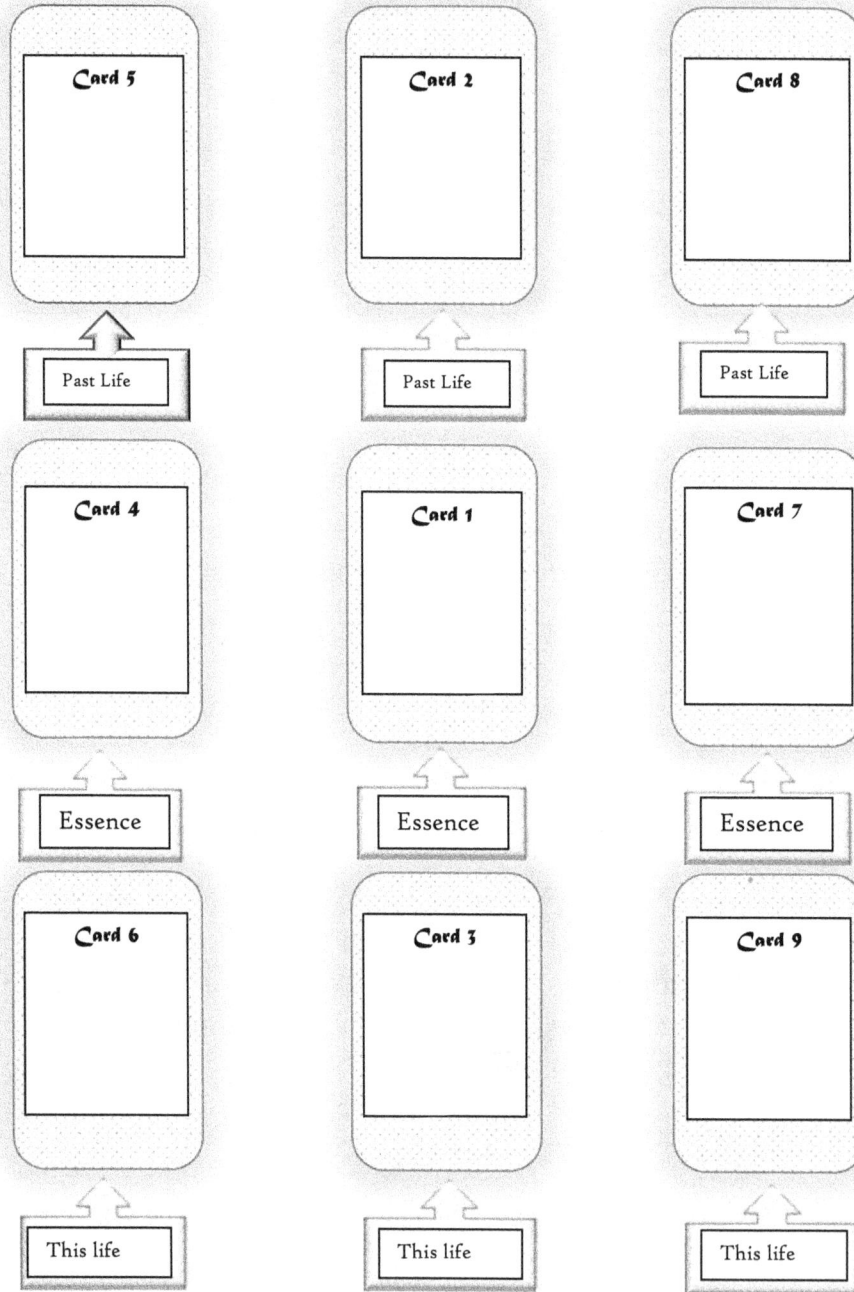

Card 5	Card 2	Card 8
Past Life	Past Life	Past Life
Card 4	Card 1	Card 7
Essence	Essence	Essence
Card 6	Card 3	Card 9
This life	This life	This life

Deconstruction/Application Day 2

	Card 1	Card 4	Card 7
My essence			
How this is connected to the past			
How it is connected to my life now			
Reflection/ Thoughts			

2.   What is the greatest insight you gained from this spread?

_____

_____

_____

3. On a scale of **1 to 10**, with **10** being "*I definitely felt connected to my spiritual essence,*" and 1 being, "*I'm not sure I had any connection to my spiritual essence,*" how connected did you feel to this spread?

         1   2   3   4   5   6   7   8   9   10

Day 3: Spiritual Essence Spread 3

For this spread, pick one essence card from Spreads 1 or 2, and pull that from the deck to place in the center of the spread. Choose one that either resonated with you strongly, or one you still have some probing questions about. For the second card, ask where you want to go in this life. We are going to dig deeper on how this essence functions for you. For the question, *Where do I want to go*, this could be applied broadly to mean a destination, personal goal, or spiritual development.

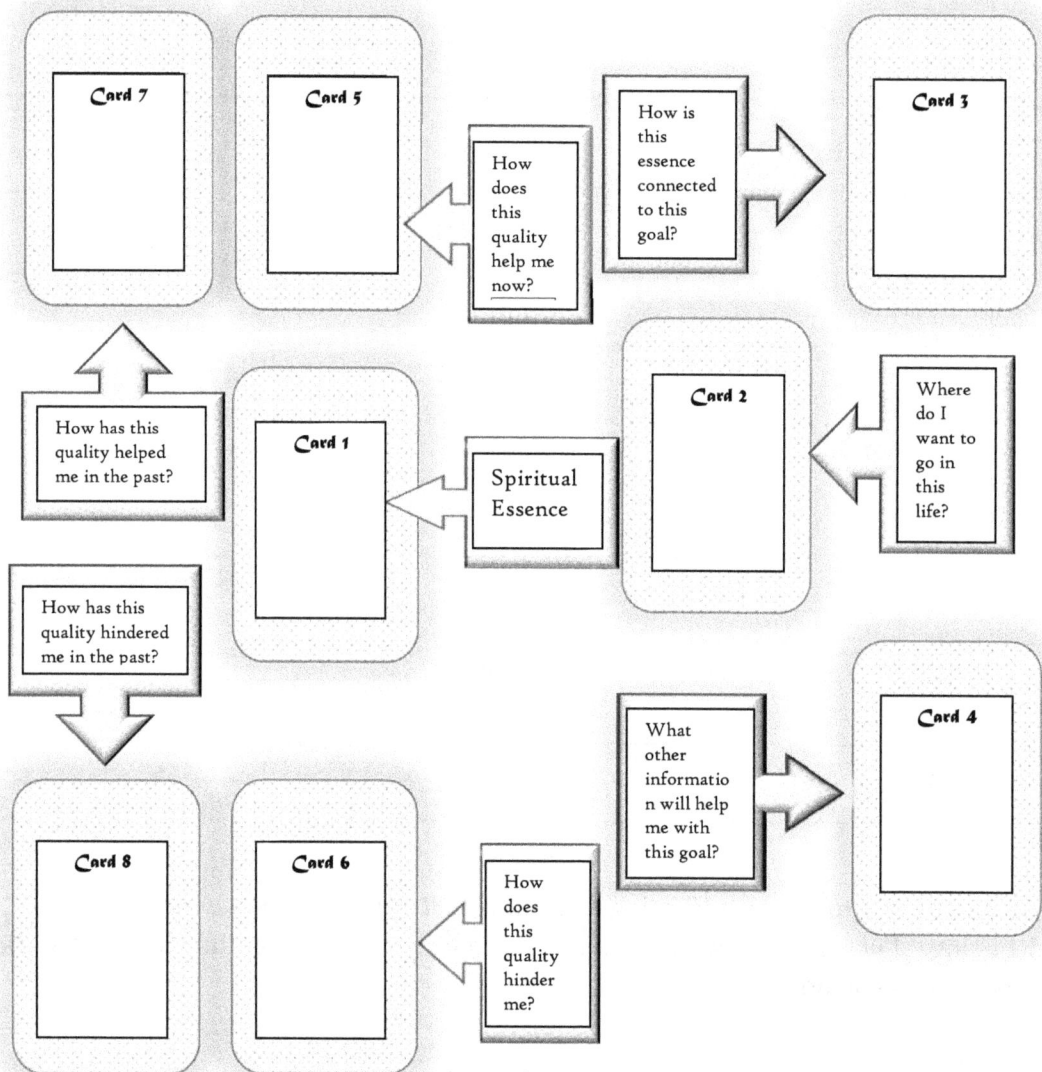

Card 7	**Card 5**	How is this essence connected to this goal?	**Card 3**
		How does this quality help me now?	
How has this quality helped me in the past?	**Card 1**	**Card 2**	Where do I want to go in this life?
		Spiritual Essence	
How has this quality hindered me in the past?			
Card 8	**Card 6**	What other information will help me with this goal?	**Card 4**
		How does this quality hinder me?	

Deconstruction/Application Day 3

1.   **The Essence**   **The Goal**

_____   _____

2. Combine **5** and **7**: **How** does this quality help me?

_____

_____

3. Combine **6** and **8**: **How** does this quality hinder me?

_____

_____

4. **What** is the <u>connection</u> between your **essence** and your **goal**?

_____

_____

5. **What** further information do you have about your **goal**? (Card 4)

_____

_____

6. What is the greatest insight you gained from this spread?

_____

_____

_____

7. On a scale of **1 to 10**, with **10** being _"I definitely felt connected to my spiritual essence,"_ and **1** being, _"I'm not sure I had any connection to my spiritual essence,"_ how connected did you feel to this spread?

    1   **2**   **3**   **4**   **5**   **6**   **7**   **8**   **9**   **10**

Days 4-6: Narrative Spreads

Narrative spreads are a key component to past life exploration. Knowing where and when, and what happened to you is the entire point! It's a good idea to develop a few running narratives as you delve into other aspects of past life exploration, such as fears and blockages. Watch carefully for repeating cards and patterns from these spreads throughout the rest of the workbook.

For *Spread 1*, you will develop a basic narrative. *Spread 2* will focus on one key event from a past life, and *Spread 3* focuses on one particular deed you committed in a past life. These deeds can be negative, (that makes sense if we are looking for information that will help us evolve) but the deed could be something good if it left a lasting impact on your energy and/or karma.

Deeds and Events Chart

Major Arcana

0-The Fool	Starting over (also points to YOU)	11-Strength	Overcoming great difficulty
1-The Magician	Manifesting; manipulator	12- The Hanged man	Stuck and unable to progress
2-The High Priestess	priestess	13- Death	Making a huge change
3-The Empress	Motherhood; creating	14- Temperance	Finding balance
4-The Emperor	Taking charge; control	15- The Devil	Addiction; obsessions
5-The Hierophant	Joining religion	16- The Tower	Big change you didn't choose
6-The Lovers	Soul mate connection with romantic partner	17- The Star	Fortune that instills your faith in your path
7-The Chariot	Driven to make something happen	18- The Moon	Secret deed or event
8- Justice	Legal troubles or events	19- The Sun	Happy times
9- The Hermit	Evolution of the soul; homebody	20- Judgment	Uncovering the truth
10- Wheel of Fortune	Major change of luck	21- The World	World recognition

Cups

Ace of Cups	Abundance of love		Eight of Cups	Abruptly walking away
Two of Cups	Making a commitment		Nine of Cups	Having a wish granted
Three of Cups	socializing		Ten of Cups	Meeting a soul mate
Four of Cups	Waiting too long		Page of Cups	Offering to help someone
Five of Cups	Losing something or someone		Knight of Cups	Being a hero
Six of Cups	Making happy memories		Queen of Cups	Showing love to everyone
Seven of Cups	Living in fantasy		King of Cups	Being emotionally dependable

Swords

Ace of Swords	Writing		Eight of Swords	imprisonment
Two of Swords	Feeling stuck and refusing to act		Nine of Swords	Look to dreams for clues
Three of Swords	heartbreak		Ten of Swords	Hitting rock bottom
Four of Swords	grieving		Page of Swords	Planning
Five of Swords	Nasty conflict		Knight of Swords	Going to battle
Six of Swords	Traveling		Queen of Swords	divorce
Seven of Swords	Stealing and significant dishonesty		King of Swords	Laying down the law; a decree

Wands

Ace of Wands	Powerful drive		Eight of Wands	communications
Two of Wands	Making plans to act		Nine of Wands	Stuck in an unpleasant situation
Three of Wands	Good karma from past lives		Ten of Wands	Managing several burdens at once
Four of Wands	Establishing a home		Page of Wands	Creating art
Five of Wands	Competitive conflict		Knight of Wands	Potent sexuality
Six of Wands	Victory and success		Queen of Wands	Leading a group
Seven of Wands	Fighting to stay on top		King of Wands	Establishing an organization

Pentacles

Ace of Pentacles	Abundance of wealth		Eight of Pentacles	Obtaining higher education
Two of Pentacles	Performance art		Nine of Pentacles	Gaining financial independence
Three of Pentacles	Working with others on a project		Ten of Pentacles	Acquiring a happy family and financial stability
Four of Pentacles	Saving money		Page of Pentacles	Caring for the earth and animals
Five of Pentacles	Losing money		Knight of Pentacles	Staying put in one location for a long time
Six of Pentacles	Donating money		Queen of Pentacles	Having children
Seven of Pentacles	Investing with hard work		King of Pentacles	Providing well for a family

Day 4: Narrative Spread 1

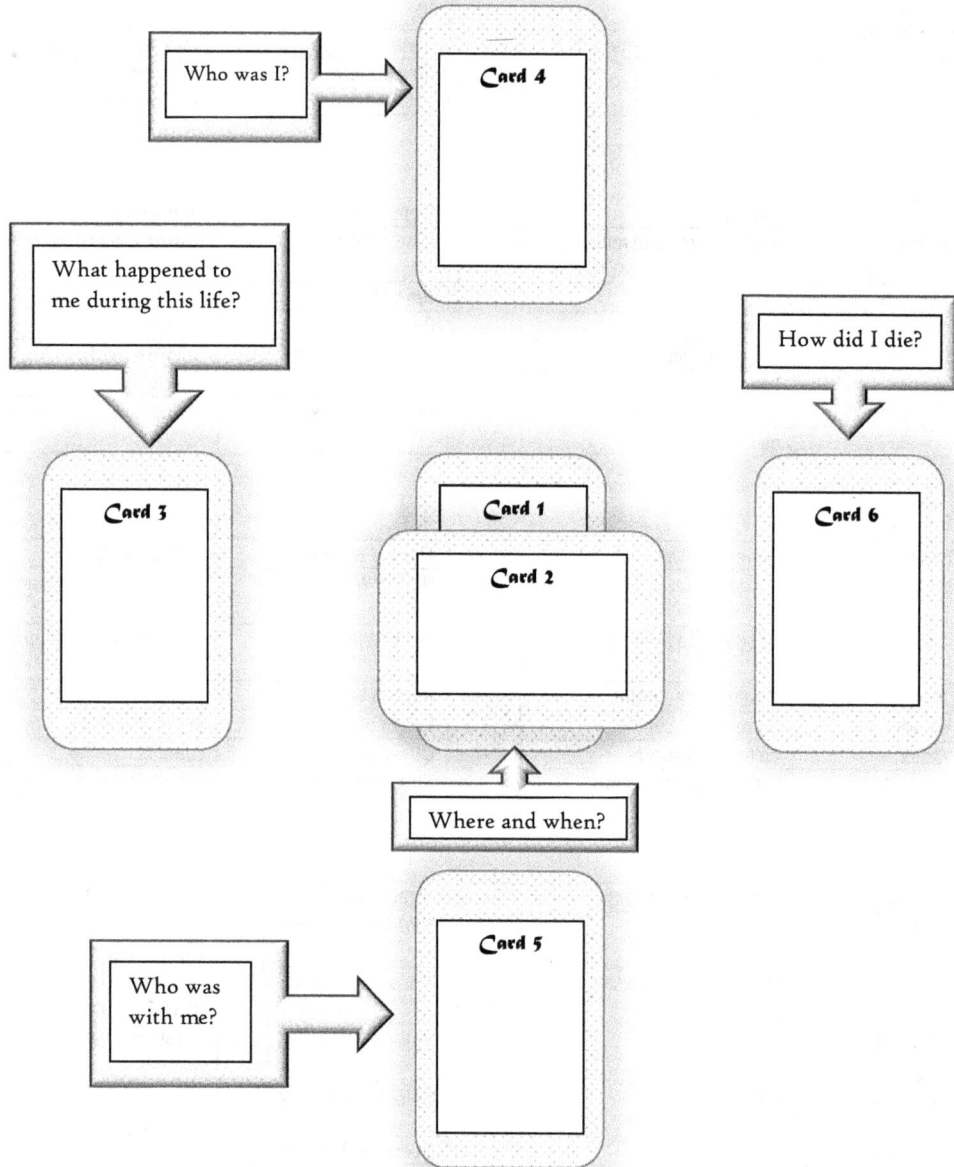

Who was I? → Card 4

What happened to me during this life? ↓ Card 3

How did I die? ↓ Card 6

Card 1

Card 2

Where and when? ↑

Who was with me? → Card 5

Deconstruction/Application Day 4

1.   **Where**   **When**

_____   _____

Note: You can use cards **1** and **2** interchangeably for place and time. Feel free to use surrounding cards for place and time as well if it makes more sense. If you are using a regular tarot deck, instead ask, _"What was going on in history during this time?"_

To construct a narrative from the cards, you may need to deviate from some of the placements if it makes more sense to do so, (for example: reading Card **3** as a place card rather than what happened). Lean heavily on images and your instinct during this process. Answer the following questions to the best of your ability. Some questions may be inconclusive.

2. **What** happened to me during this life?

_____

_____

3. **Who** was I?

_____

4. **Who** was with me? (**Note**: if you pull "brother" then a brother you have now was with you then).

_____

5. **How** did I die?

_____

6. On a scale of **1 to 10**, with **10** being _"This was a fully formed narrative that resonated with me completely,"_ and **1** being, _"I was not able to construct a narrative from this spread,"_ how connected did you feel to this spread?

      1   2   3   4   5   6   7   8   9   10

Day 5: Narrative Spread 2

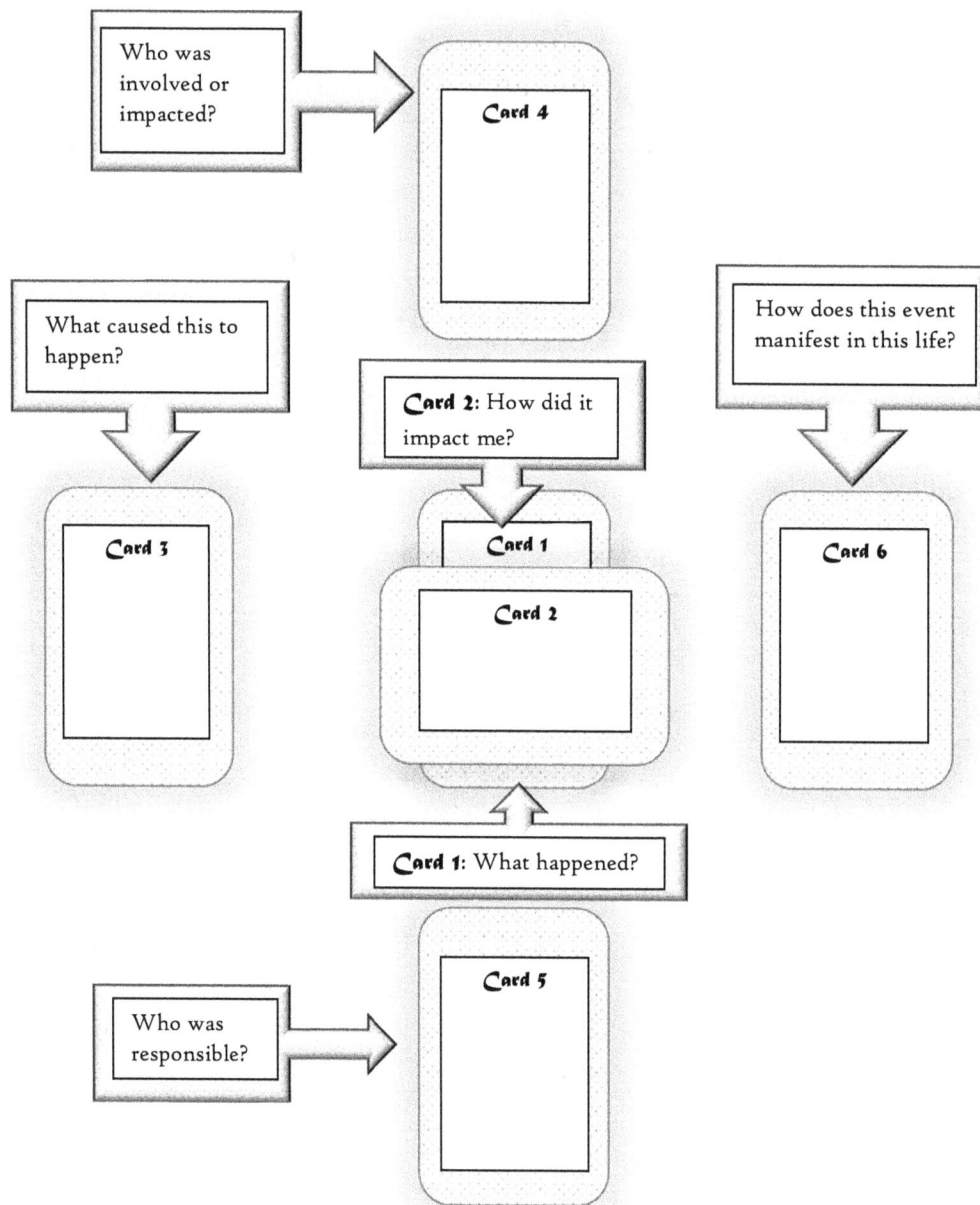

| Who was involved or impacted? | → | **Card 4** |

| What caused this to happen? | | How does this event manifest in this life? |

Card 2: How did it impact me?

Card 3

Card 1

Card 2

Card 6

Card 1: What happened?

| Who was responsible? | → | **Card 5** |

Deconstruction/Application Day 5

1. **What happened**   **How it impacted me**

_____   _____

To construct a narrative from the cards, you may need to deviate from some of the placements if it makes more sense to do so. Lean heavily on images and your instinct during this process. Answer the following questions to the best of your ability. Some questions may be inconclusive.

2. **What** caused this to happen?

_____

_____

3. **Who** was involved or impacted?

_____

4. **Who** was responsible?

_____

5. **How** does this event manifest in this life?

_____

_____

_____

6. On a scale of **1 to 10**, with **10** being _"I am fully able to see how this narrative impacts me now,"_ and **1** being, _"I'm unsure how this narrative impacts me now,"_ how connected did you feel to this spread?

     1   **2**   **3**   **4**   **5**   **6**   **7**   **8**   **9**   **10**

Day 6: Narrative Spread 3

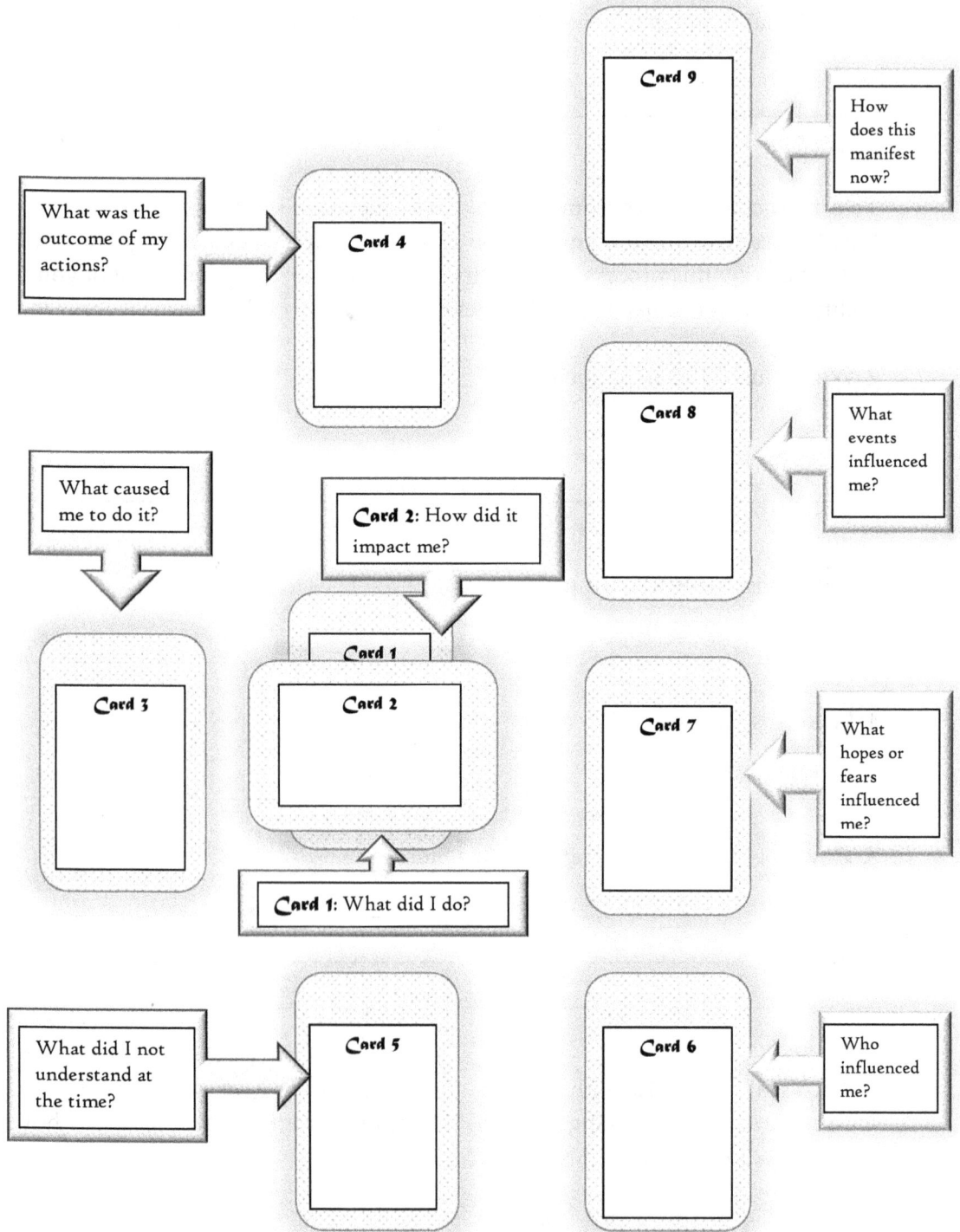

Card 9

How does this manifest now?

What was the outcome of my actions?

Card 4

Card 8

What events influenced me?

What caused me to do it?

Card 2: How did it impact me?

Card 1

Card 3

Card 2

Card 7

What hopes or fears influenced me?

Card 1: What did I do?

What did I not understand at the time?

Card 5

Card 6

Who influenced me?

Deconstruction/Application Day 6

1.   **What did I do?**   **How it impacted me**

_____   _____

To construct a narrative from the cards, you may need to deviate from some of the placements if it makes more sense to do so. Lean heavily on images and your instinct during this process.

2. **What** caused me to do it?

_____

3. **What** was the <u>outcome</u> of my actions?

_____

4. **What** did I not understand at the time?

_____

5. **How** does this event manifest in this life?

_____

Who influenced me	
What hopes or fears influenced me?	
What events influenced me?	

6. On a scale of **1 to 10**, with **10** being _"I am fully able to see how this narrative impacts me now,"_ and **1** being, _"I'm unsure how this narrative impacts me now,"_ how connected did you feel to this spread?

1   2   3   4   5   6   7   8   9   10

Days 7-9: Spiritual Blockage Spreads

A spiritual blockage is any kind of barrier in your current life that has a spiritual root. Something you have done or experienced in a past life is the true reason for your psychology and behavior. This concept is similar to fears or phobias, but the distinction is that the blockage is the "thing in the way." Blockages tend to be greater in capacity than a fear or a phobia and are typically energetically stronger. It's much tougher to break a blockage because you have been working through this adversarial energy through several lifetimes.

Spread 1 will help you identify at least one blockage, *Spread 2* leads you to your next step in progress towards working through that blockage, and *Spread 3* will show you what to look for as indicators of success on your journey towards absolving that particular blockage.

Spiritual Blockage Reference Guide

Major Arcana

0-The Fool	Unwillingness to venture out	**11-Strength**	Deep wounds
1-The Magician	Denying your inherent power	**12- The Hanged man**	Directionless
2-The High Priestess	Too much observing without enough action	**13- Death**	Can't adjust to change
3-The Empress	Blocked creativity	**14- Temperance**	Struggles with routine and healthy habits
4-The Emperor	Too demanding	**15- The Devil**	Addictions and obsessions
5-The Hierophant	Loyal to religion even when it is wayward	**16- The Tower**	Let's others decide your fate too willingly
6-The Lovers	Unable to make critical choices	**17- The Star**	Struggles to believe in the path
7-The Chariot	Tramples over others to get what you want	**18- The Moon**	Can't see your own spirit clearly
8- Justice	Black and white thinking	**19- The Sun**	Overly concerned with recognition
9- The Hermit	Misses interpersonal connection with others	**20- Judgment**	Fears God
10- Wheel of Fortune	Doesn't plan enough	**21- The World**	Too worldly and disconnected from spirit

Cups

Ace of Cups	Absence of love		Eight of Cups	wanderlust
Two of Cups	Lack of commitment		Nine of Cups	Too focused on the future
Three of Cups	Struggle to maintain a friendship (just one)		Ten of Cups	Allows emotional state to dictate reality
Four of Cups	Never satisfied		Page of Cups	Unsure how to love
Five of Cups	Make decisions based on fear		Knight of Cups	Overly charitable with time
Six of Cups	Family connections need healing		Queen of Cups	Does good deeds at the expense of self
Seven of Cups	Indulge in fantasy rather than living your life		King of Cups	Feels responsible for others' feelings

Swords

Ace of Swords	Being honest with yourself		Eight of Swords	Won't face your fears
Two of Swords	Avoidance		Nine of Swords	Anxiety rooted in past lives
Three of Swords	Broken heart rooted in past lives		Ten of Swords	Struggling to start over
Four of Swords	illnesses		Page of Swords	Lack of planning
Five of Swords	Dominating behavior		Knight of Swords	Too impulsive
Six of Swords	Inability to move on from loss or heartbreak		Queen of Swords	Overly judgmental
Seven of Swords	Dishonesty		King of Swords	Overly analytical

Wands

Ace of Wands	Lack of drive		Eight of Wands	Need to communicate
Two of Wands	Too much planning without enough action		Nine of Wands	Inferiority complex
Three of Wands	Waiting on returns		Ten of Wands	Easily overwhelmed
Four of Wands	Don't want to sacrifice stability		Page of Wands	Ignores red flags
Five of Wands	Overly competitive		Knight of Wands	Sex driven
Six of Wands	Tunnel vision on achievement		Queen of Wands	vanity
Seven of Wands	Martyr mentality		King of Wands	False persona

Pentacles

Ace of Pentacles	Focused on money		Eight of Pentacles	Too much focus on the next thing without focus on now
Two of Pentacles	Takes on too much		Nine of Pentacles	Too independent
Three of Pentacles	Feeling more capable than others		Ten of Pentacles	Too comfortable
Four of Pentacles	Greed and stinginess		Page of Pentacles	Don't act on good ideas
Five of Pentacles	Poverty mentality		Knight of Pentacles	Unwilling to change
Six of Pentacles	Relies too much on others		Queen of Pentacles	Identity attached to who you are for others
Seven of Pentacles	Unwilling to invest time and energy		King of Pentacles	Identity attached to wealth

Day 7: Spiritual Blockage Spread 1

For this spread, you are working to identify what your spiritual blockages may be and looking for insight that will help you form breakthroughs. Spiritual blockages are deep psychological beliefs or fears that are preventing your spiritual progression.

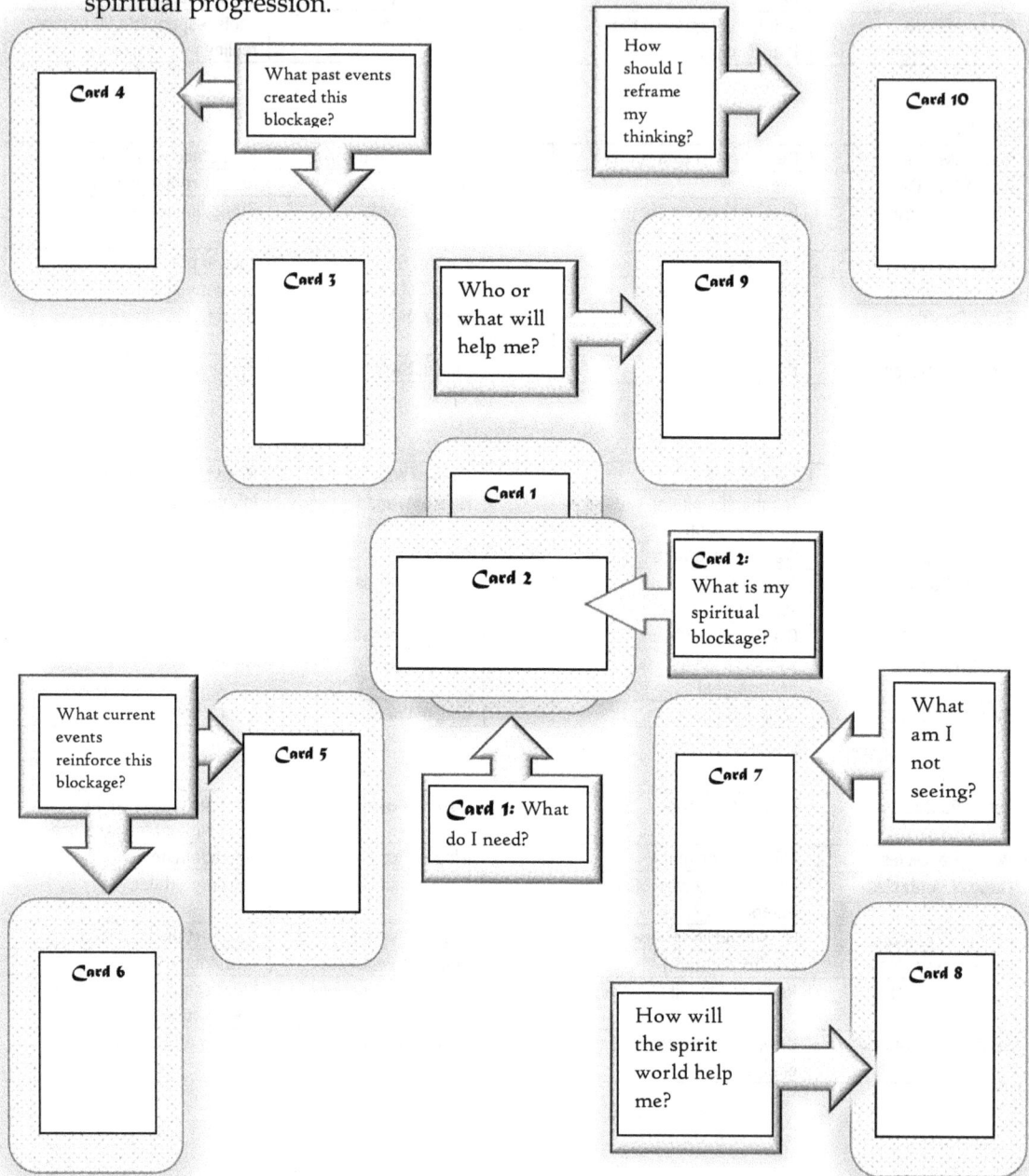

Card 4

What past events created this blockage?

How should I reframe my thinking?

Card 10

Card 3

Who or what will help me?

Card 9

Card 1

Card 2

Card 2: What is my spiritual blockage?

What current events reinforce this blockage?

Card 5

Card 1: What do I need?

Card 7

What am I not seeing?

Card 6

How will the spirit world help me?

Card 8

Deconstruction/Application Day 7

1.   **What do I need?**   **What is my spiritual blockage?**

_____   _____

2. **What** past life events created this blockage?

_____

_____

3. **What** current life events reinforced this blockage?

_____

_____

4. **What** am I not seeing?

_____

5. **How** will the spirit world help me?

_____

6. **Who** or **what** in the physical world will help me?

_____

7. **How** should I reframe my thinking?

_____

_____

_____

8. On a scale of **1 to 10**, with **10** being *"I now have more clarity about my spiritual blockage and how to address it,"* and **1** being, *"I have no clarity about my spiritual blockages"* how connected did you feel to this spread?

1   2   3   4   5   6   7   8   9   10

Day 8: Spiritual Blockage Spread 2

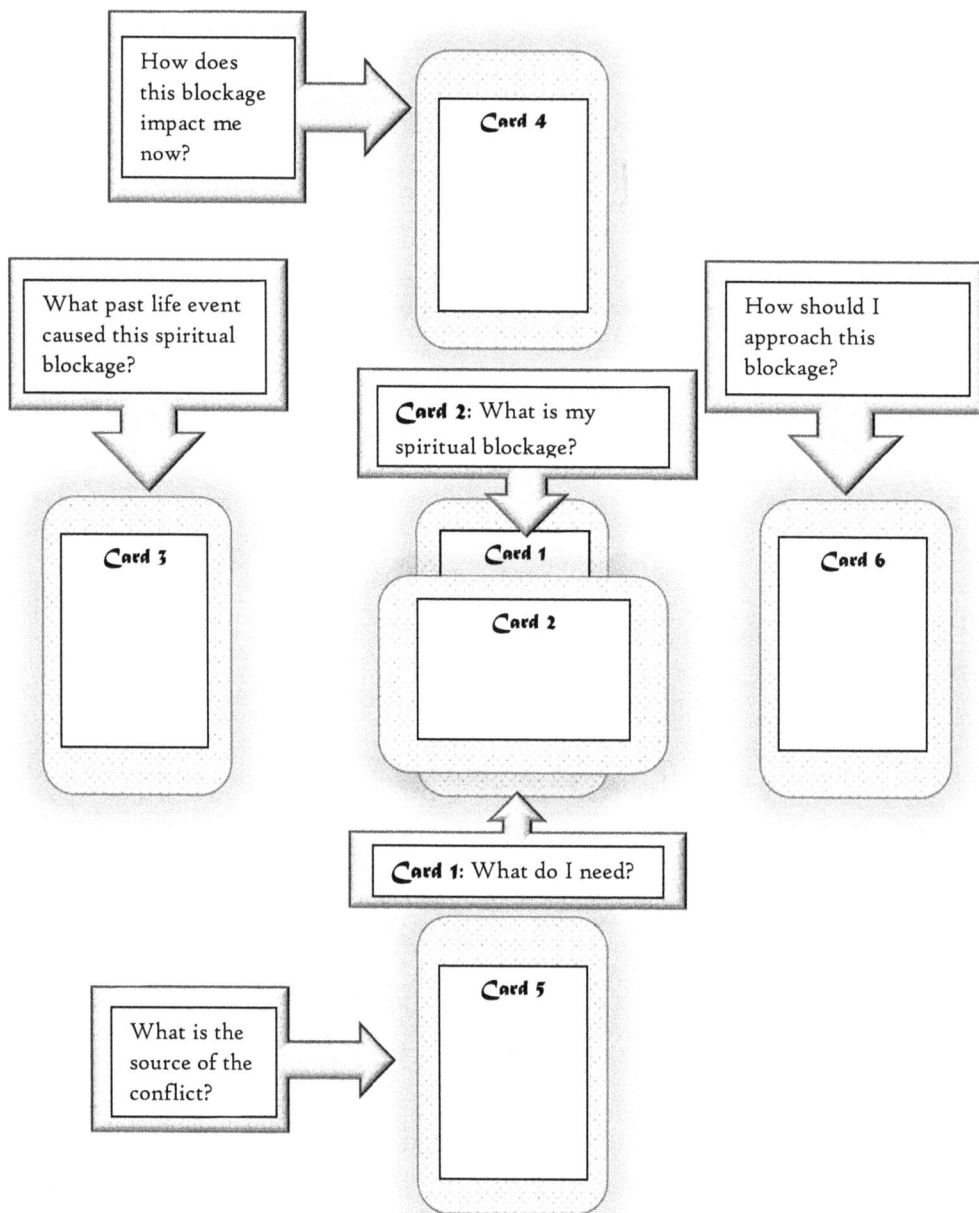

How does this blockage impact me now?

Card 4

What past life event caused this spiritual blockage?

Card 3

Card 2: What is my spiritual blockage?

Card 1

Card 2

How should I approach this blockage?

Card 6

Card 1: What do I need?

What is the source of the conflict?

Card 5

Deconstruction/Application Day 8

1. **What do I need?**   **What is my spiritual blockage?**

_____ _____

2. **What** past life <u>event</u> created this blockage?

_____

_____

3. **How** does this blockage impact me now?

_____

_____

4. **What** is the <u>source</u> of the conflict?

_____

_____

5. **How** should I approach this blockage?

_____

6. Was there any repetition from the previous spread? Note either repeating cards or repeating energy/messages

_____

_____

7. Greatest insight from this spread:

_____

_____

_____

8. On a scale of **1 to 10**, with **10** being "_I now have more clarity about my spiritual blockage and how to address it,_" and **1** being, "_I have no clarity about my spiritual blockages_" how connected did you feel to this spread?

   1 2 3 4 5 6 7 8 9 10

Day 9: Spiritual Blockage Spread 3

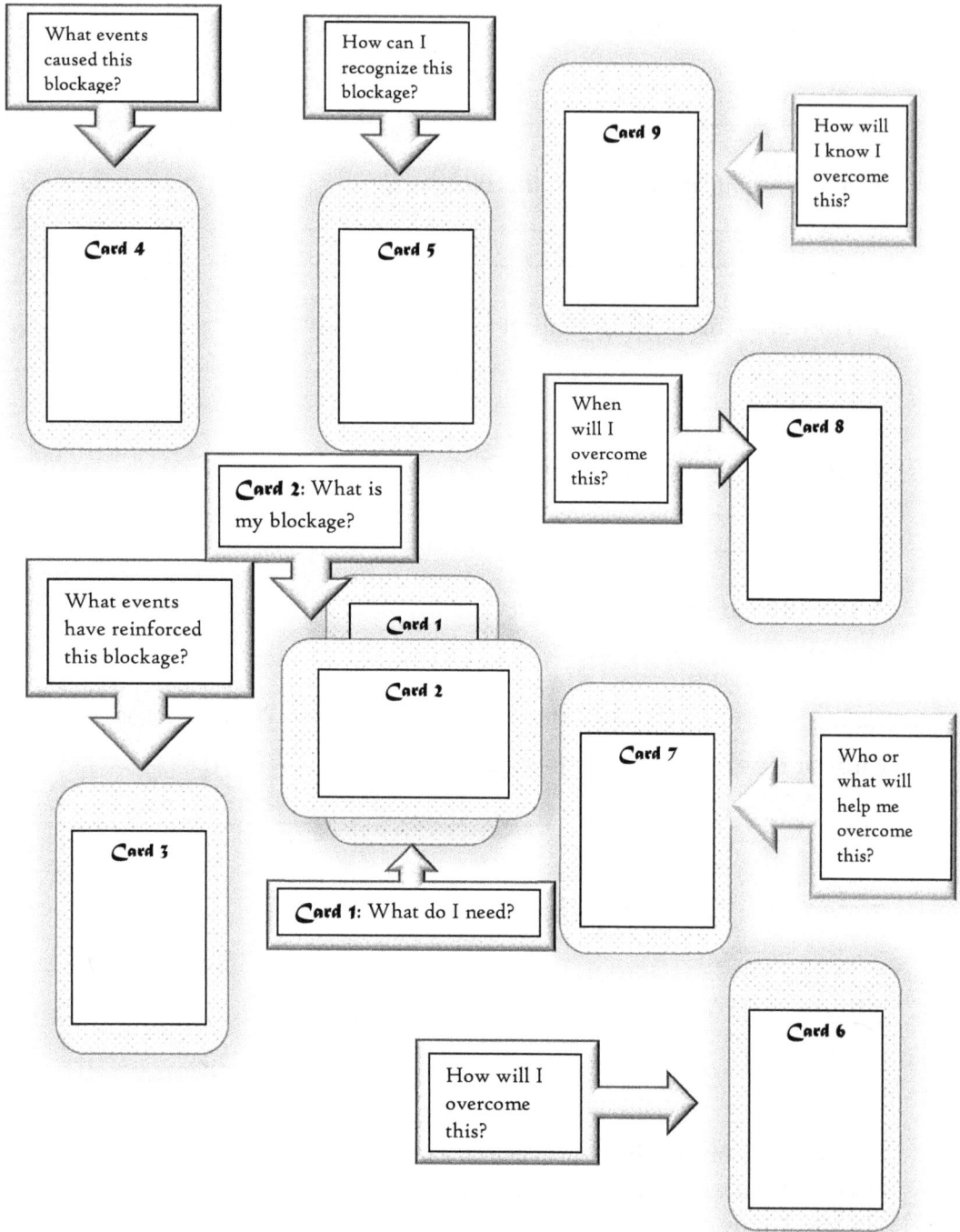

What events caused this blockage?

How can I recognize this blockage?

Card 9

How will I know I overcome this?

Card 4

Card 5

When will I overcome this?

Card 8

Card 2: What is my blockage?

What events have reinforced this blockage?

Card 1

Card 2

Card 7

Who or what will help me overcome this?

Card 3

Card 1: What do I need?

How will I overcome this?

Card 6

Deconstruction/Application Day 9

1. **What do I need?**   **What is my spiritual blockage?**

_____   _____

2. **What** event <u>caused</u> this blockage?

_____

_____

3. **What** event <u>reinforced</u> this blockage?

_____

_____

4. **How** can I <u>recognize</u> this blockage?

_____

_____

5. **How** will I <u>overcome</u> this blockage?

_____

6. **Who** or **what** will help me?

_____

_____

7. **When** or **how** will I know I've overcome this blockage?

_____

_____

_____

8. On a scale of **1 to 10**, with **10** being _"I now have more clarity about my spiritual blockage and how to address it,"_ and **1** being, _"I have no clarity about my spiritual blockages"_ how connected did you feel to this spread?

   1   2   3   4   5   6   7   8   9   10

Days 10-12: Relationship Spreads

Relationships are a key aspect of the incarnation experience. Not only do we have goals and unique paths for this life, but we also continue important bonds and sometimes agree to help one another on our paths. We sometimes contract to help our loved one grow and evolve in certain scenarios. Sometimes, we give someone another chance to right a wrong committed against us, and vice versa. Identifying your soul contracts with others can help facilitate the growth between you, and can bring peace in situations where the outcome is less than ideal. The pain we cause each other is reconciled through God once we leave this earth, but the evolution of our soul is dependent on our choices and growth we accomplish while we are here. Hence, your soul contracts are a key part of nurturing your soul in the direction you want to go.

Refer to the chart below for specific interpretations of soul contracts for each card. You can interpret the cards differently if it makes sense to do so. The chart is designed to give you a start in how to frame your thinking.

Soul Contract Reference Guide

Major Arcana

0-The Fool	Journey together	11-Strength	Heal a deep wound between you
1-The Magician	Practice magic together	12- The Hanged man	One helps the other with a spiritual blockage
2-The High Priestess	Develop intuition together	13- Death	One awaits the other after death
3-The Empress	Care for children together	14- Temperance	Create harmony in the home
4-The Emperor	Provide structure together	15- The Devil	Unhealthy bond
5-The Hierophant	Share religious beliefs	16- The Tower	One helps the other with a spiritual breakthrough
6-The Lovers	Promise to find each other	17- The Star	One deeply loves and supports the other
7-The Chariot	One helps other overcome impulses	18- The Moon	Subconscious connection even when not together
8- Justice	Settle a karmic debt between you	19- The Sun	Promise to care about the other's happiness
9- The Hermit	One is the other's spiritual teacher	20- Judgment	One reminds the other of spiritual truth
10- Wheel of Fortune	Share a full life together	21- The World	Promise to heal the world together

Cups

Ace of Cups	Loved each other before	Eight of Cups	Not a lifetime commitment
Two of Cups	Lifetime commitment	Nine of Cups	One fulfills another's wish or physical need
Three of Cups	Three people connected through past life; three-way bond	Ten of Cups	Bond offers secure emotional fulfillment
Four of Cups	Promise to wake the other up spiritually	Page of Cups	One will charitably love the other
Five of Cups	Promise to comfort during loss	Knight of Cups	True friendship
Six of Cups	Deep family bond	Queen of Cups	One will care for the other when sick
Seven of Cups	Inspire each other	King of Cups	Love between you will never be questioned

Swords

Ace of Swords	One will show the other the truth	Eight of Swords	One will work on being less controlling/imprisoning the other
Two of Swords	One will lead the other from blindness	Nine of Swords	Work on healing a wound from the past
Three of Swords	One will attempt to heal a past broken heart	Ten of Swords	One is working on respecting the other's autonomy
Four of Swords	One will retreat from the other to enable them to grow	Page of Swords	Making plans for the future together
Five of Swords	One is going to try to be less abusive	Knight of Swords	Resolving a past conflict
Six of Swords	Travel together	Queen of Swords	Attempt to avoid divorce
Seven of Swords	One is going to try to be more honest and trustworthy	King of Swords	One is working on being less cold

Wands

Ace of Wands	One will inspire the other to live better	Eight of Wands	Develop better communication
Two of Wands	Plan a business together	Nine of Wands	One helps the other with limitations
Three of Wands	Create a family	Ten of Wands	Ease each other's burdens
Four of Wands	Domestic contract	Page of Wands	One will deliver a spiritual message to the other
Five of Wands	Working to compete less with each other	Knight of Wands	Sexual connection
Six of Wands	Achieve a victory together	Queen of Wands	One creates art for/about the other
Seven of Wands	Fight enemies together	King of Wands	One is key in the other's professional development

Pentacles

Ace of Pentacles	One will teach the other to manifest	Eight of Pentacles	One teaches the other
Two of Pentacles	Contract involves performance art	Nine of Pentacles	One helps the other with independence
Three of Pentacles	Worked together to create something significant	Ten of Pentacles	Happy family
Four of Pentacles	One helps the other with spending habits	Page of Pentacles	Work on a project together
Five of Pentacles	Suffer together	Knight of Pentacles	One won't abandon the other
Six of Pentacles	Charity within the relationship	Queen of Pentacles	Nurture each other
Seven of Pentacles	One is waiting for the other to fulfill karma	King of Pentacles	Provide for each other

Day 10: Relationship Spread 1 General Karmic

Use this spread to look at the history of a relationship with someone that has not been very healthy or uplifting to you personally.

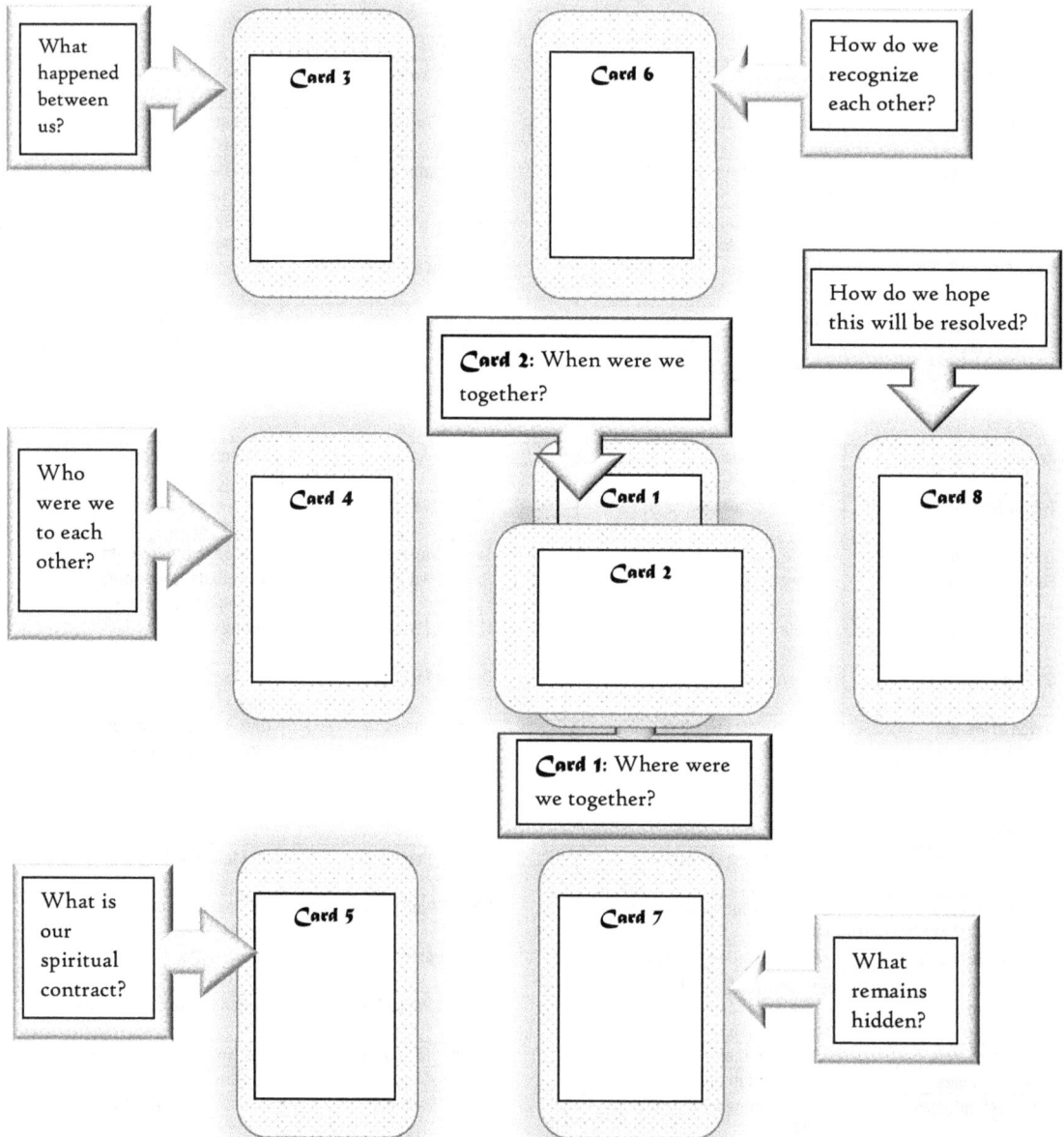

| What happened between us? | → | **Card 3** | | **Card 6** | ← | How do we recognize each other? |

How do we hope this will be resolved?

Card 2: When were we together?

| Who were we to each other? | ⇒ | **Card 4** | **Card 1** | **Card 8** |

Card 2

Card 1: Where were we together?

| What is our spiritual contract? | ⇒ | **Card 5** | **Card 7** | ← | What remains hidden? |

Deconstruction/Application Day 10

1.   **Where**   **When**

_____   _____

Note: You can use cards **1** and **2** interchangeably for place and time. Feel free to use surrounding cards for place and time as well if it makes more sense. If you are using a regular tarot deck, instead ask, _"What was going on in history during this time?"_

Name or initials of the person I'm reading on: _____

2. **What** happened between us?

_____

3. **Who** were we to each other?

_____

4. **What** is our spiritual contract?

_____

5. **How** do we recognize each other?

_____

6. **What** remains hidden?

_____

7. **How** do we hope this will be resolved?

_____

8. On a scale of **1 to 10**, with **10** being _"I've gained substantial spiritual insight into my relationship with this person,"_ and **1** being, _"I have gained no spiritual insight into this relationship,"_ how connected did you feel to this spread?

       1   **2**   **3**   **4**   **5**   **6**   **7**   **8**   **9**   **10**

Day 11: Relationship Spread 2 Family/Friend

Use this spread for a healthy/happy relationship. This can be used for a romantic relationship as well, but better suited for a long-term romantic relationship.

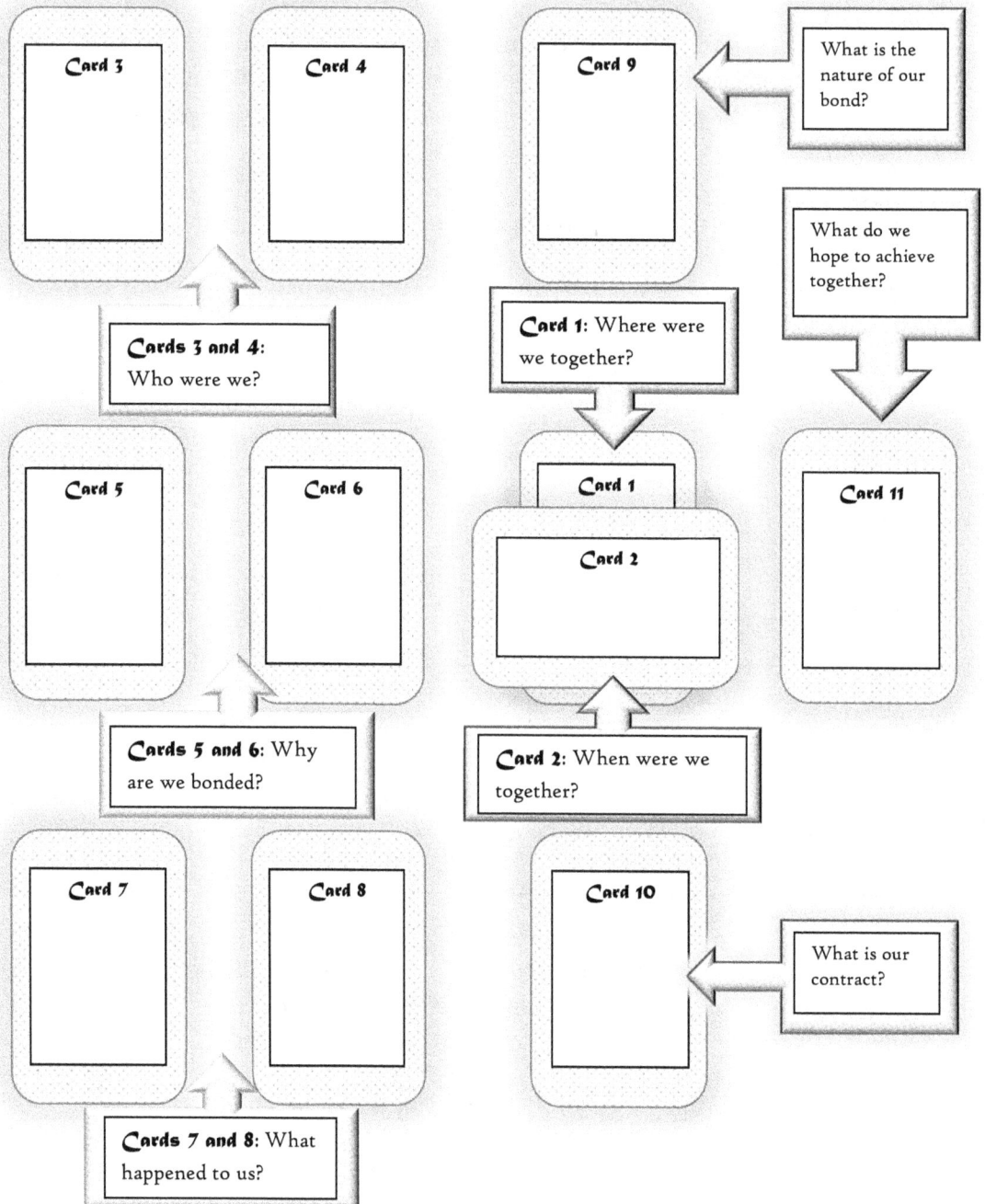

Card 3

Card 4

Card 9

What is the nature of our bond?

Cards 3 and 4: Who were we?

Card 1: Where were we together?

What do we hope to achieve together?

Card 5

Card 6

Card 1

Card 2

Card 11

Cards 5 and 6: Why are we bonded?

Card 2: When were we together?

Card 7

Card 8

Card 10

What is our contract?

Cards 7 and 8: What happened to us?

Deconstruction/Application Day 11

1.   **Where**   **When**

_____   _____

Note: You can use cards 1 and 2 interchangeably for place and time. Feel free to use surrounding cards for place and time as well if it makes more sense. If you are using a regular tarot deck, instead ask, *"What was going on in history during this time?"*

Name or initials of the person I'm reading on: _____

2. **Who** were we to each other?
_____

3. **Why** are we bonded?
_____

4. **What** happened to us?
_____

5. **What** is the nature of our bond?
_____

6.   **What** is our contract?
_____

7.   **What** do we hope to accomplish together?

_____

8.   On a scale of **1 to 10**, with **10** being *"I've gained substantial spiritual insight into my relationship with this person,"* and **1** being, *"I have gained no spiritual insight into this relationship,"* how connected did you feel to this spread?

         1   2   3   4   5   6   7   8   9   10

Day 12: Relationship Spread 3 Romantic

Use this spread for a short-term romantic relationship, or a romantic relationship with serious issues/unhealthy dynamics.

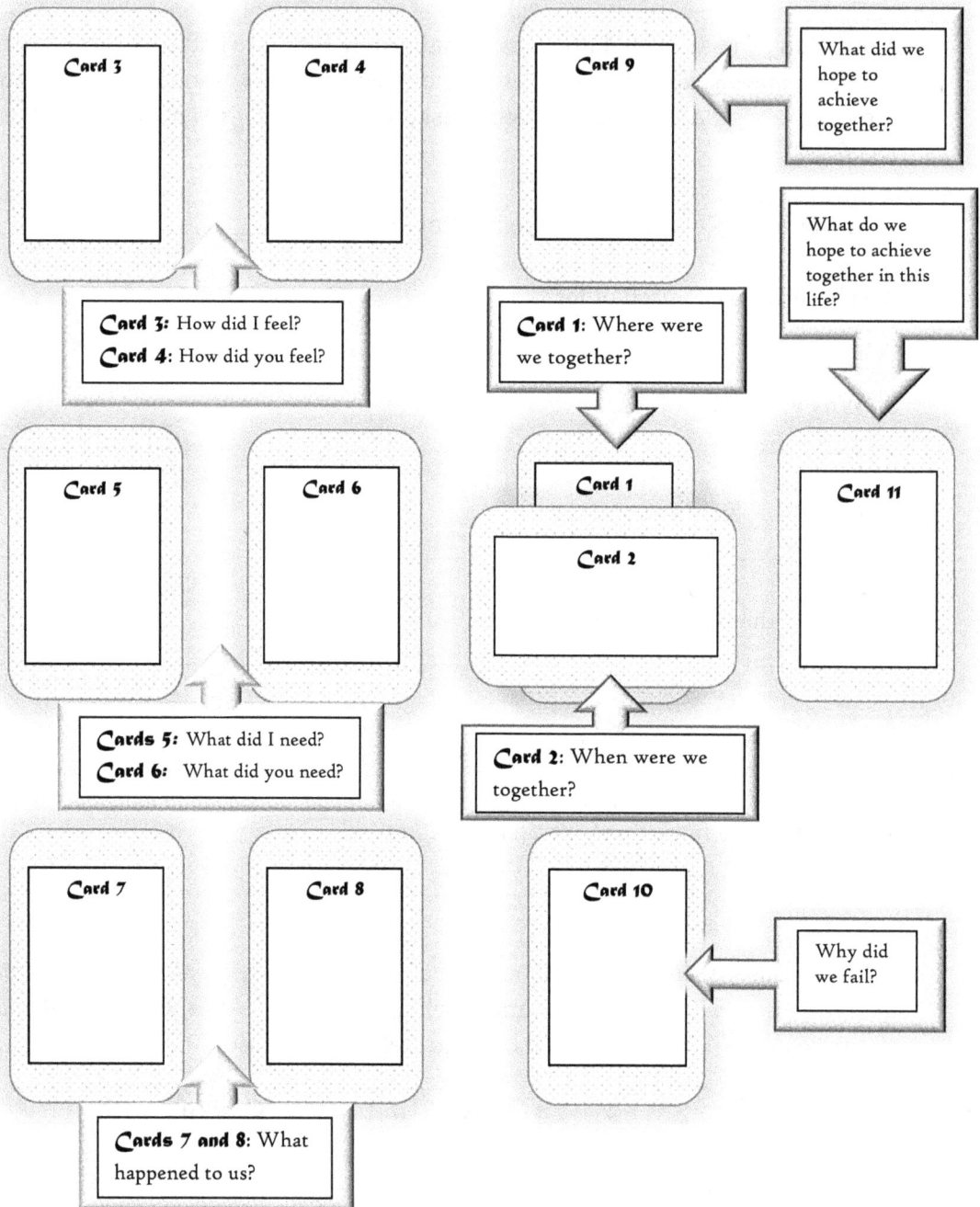

Card 3

Card 4

Card 9

What did we hope to achieve together?

Card 3: How did I feel?

Card 4: How did you feel?

Card 1: Where were we together?

What do we hope to achieve together in this life?

Card 5

Card 6

Card 1

Card 2

Card 11

Cards 5: What did I need?

Card 6: What did you need?

Card 2: When were we together?

Card 7

Card 8

Card 10

Why did we fail?

Cards 7 and 8: What happened to us?

Deconstruction/Application Day 12

1.   **Where**   **When**

_____   _____

Note: You can use cards 1 and 2 interchangeably for place and time. Feel free to use surrounding cards for place and time as well if it makes more sense. If you are using a regular tarot deck, instead ask, *"What was going on in history during this time?"*

Name or initials of the person I'm reading on: _____

How I felt about you in this relationship	How you felt about me in this relationship
What I needed from the relationship	What you needed from the relationship

2. **What** did we hope to achieve together in this past life?

_____

3. **Why** did we fail?

_____

4. **What** do we hope to achieve together in this life?

_____

5. On a scale of **1 to 10**, with **10** being *"I've gained substantial spiritual insight into my relationship with this person,"* and **1** being, *"I have gained no spiritual insight into this relationship,"* how connected did you feel to this spread?

    1   2   3   4   5   6   7   8   9   10

Days 13-15: Phobias and Fears Spreads

Being able to isolate and identify past life events that have either caused or reinforced certain fears can be a powerful tool for healing and strength. When we understand the "why" about our fears, then we can begin to process them to engage in interior dialogues with ourselves. That process will facilitate our mastery of our own minds and give us the best chance of living a successful life.

Spread 1 is designed to help you identify a fear. Sometimes, we aren't fully conscious of what we are afraid of. Sometimes we dance around our fears and refuse to admit me have them because we know logically that they aren't rational. So *Spread 1* can aid in gaining that clarity.

Spread 2 is designed to find the root cause of a fear once it has been identified, and *Spread 3* is designed to focus on strategies for overcoming a fear.

Phobias and Fears Reference Guide

Major Arcana

0-The Fool	Afraid of starting over	11-Strength	Afraid of working through trauma
1-The Magician	Afraid of tapping into your own power	12- The Hanged man	Unfinished business
2-The High Priestess	Afraid of the divine feminine	13- Death	Afraid of the unknown
3-The Empress	Afraid of your mother or afraid of being your mother	14- Temperance	Afraid of monotony
4-The Emperor	Afraid of your father or afraid of being your father	15- The Devil	Afraid of addiction or commitment
5-The Hierophant	Afraid of being lost in mediocrity by meeting expectations	16- The Tower	Afraid of the unknown
6-The Lovers	Afraid of emotional intimacy	17- The Star	Afraid of being lost
7-The Chariot	Afraid of pursuing your dreams	18- The Moon	Afraid of the spirit world
8- Justice	Afraid of legal troubles	19- The Sun	Afraid of allowing yourself to feel happy
9- The Hermit	Afraid of losing your individuality	20- Judgment	Afraid of judgment; others and/or God
10- Wheel of Fortune	Afraid of change	21- The World	Afraid of public ridicule

Cups

Ace of Cups	Afraid of giving/receiving love	Eight of Cups	Afraid of being abandoned
Two of Cups	Afraid of commitment	Nine of Cups	Afraid to dream
Three of Cups	Social anxiety	Ten of Cups	Afraid to take emotional risks
Four of Cups	Afraid of losing yourself	Page of Cups	Afraid to offer yourself
Five of Cups	Afraid of losing a loved one	Knight of Cups	Afraid to let your emotions lead
Six of Cups	Afraid of the future	Queen of Cups	Afraid of losing yourself to love
Seven of Cups	Afraid to live in the now	King of Cups	Afraid of emotionally supporting someone

Swords

Ace of Swords	Afraid of the truth	Eight of Swords	Afraid to test boundaries
Two of Swords	Afraid to take action	Nine of Swords	Afraid of the future
Three of Swords	Afraid to love again	Ten of Swords	Afraid of losing everything
Four of Swords	Afraid of illness	Page of Swords	Afraid of not being prepared
Five of Swords	Afraid of conflict	Knight of Swords	Afraid to go to battle
Six of Swords	Scared of water	Queen of Swords	Afraid of putting an end to something
Seven of Swords	Afraid of being taken advantage of	King of Swords	Afraid to set boundaries

Wands

Ace of Wands	Lack of trust in creative ability	Eight of Wands	Afraid of direct communication
Two of Wands	Lack of strategy	Nine of Wands	Claustrophobia
Three of Wands	Afraid of adding a third party to a dynamic	Ten of Wands	Afraid of mounting debt (fiscal or karmic)
Four of Wands	Afraid of instability	Page of Wands	Afraid to share your art
Five of Wands	Afraid to compete	Knight of Wands	Afraid to have ambition
Six of Wands	Afraid of accomplishment	Queen of Wands	Afraid of the public eye
Seven of Wands	Paranoid about theft	King of Wands	Afraid to lead

Pentacles

Ace of Pentacles	Afraid of never having abundance	Eight of Pentacles	Afraid to pursue accomplishment
Two of Pentacles	Afraid to perform	Nine of Pentacles	Afraid of being alone
Three of Pentacles	Afraid to commit to projects or organizations	Ten of Pentacles	Afraid you won't climb out of hardship
Four of Pentacles	Afraid of not having enough money	Page of Pentacles	Afraid of nature (spiders, snakes, tornados, etc)
Five of Pentacles	Afraid of destitution	Knight of Pentacles	Afraid of changing the routine
Six of Pentacles	Afraid of being conned	Queen of Pentacles	Afraid of pregnancy or delivery; afraid of being too worldly
Seven of Pentacles	Afraid investment won't pay off	King of Pentacles	Afraid you can't provide

Day 13: Phobias and Fears Spread 1

This spread is best for identifying a fear rather than looking more deeply at a fear you are aware of.

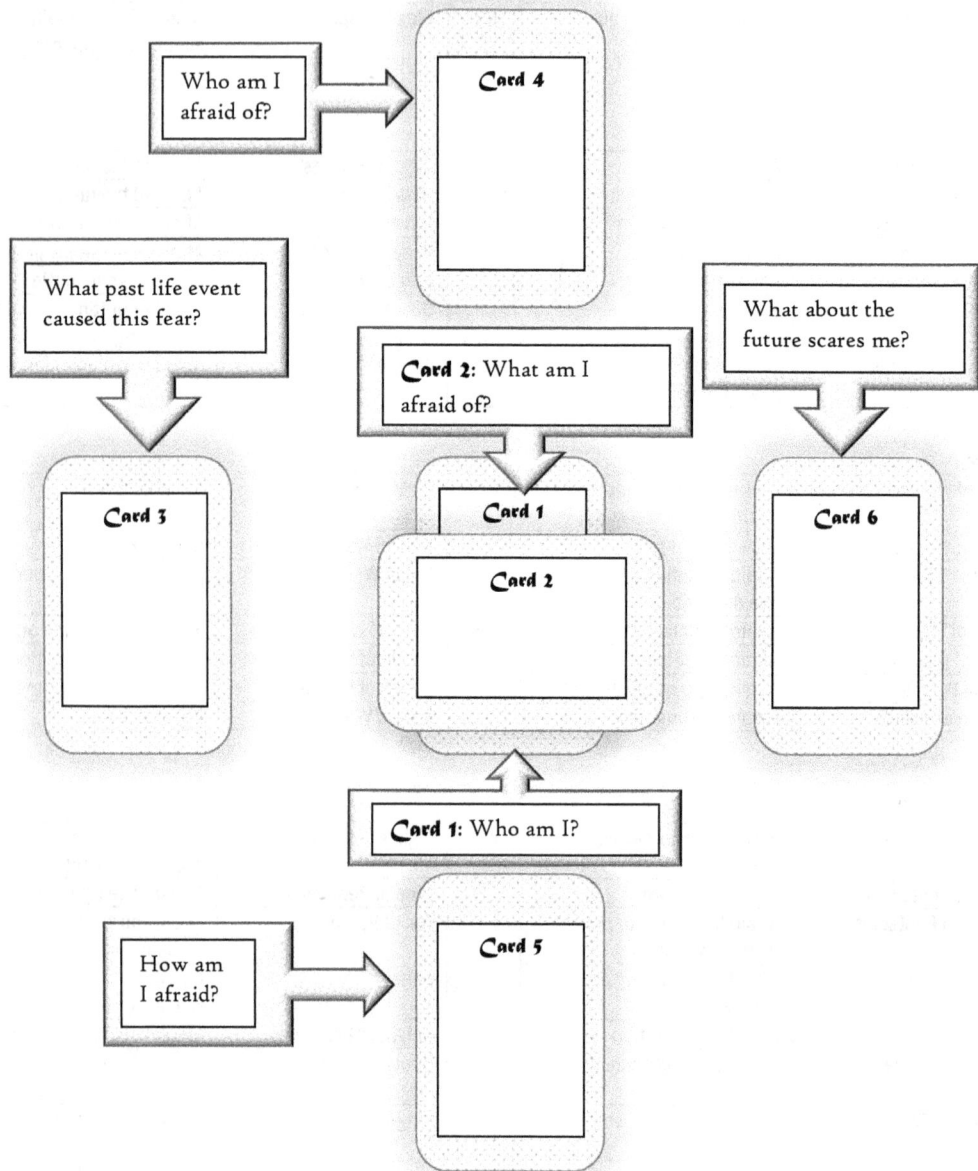

Who am I afraid of? → Card 4

What past life event caused this fear? ↓

Card 2: What am I afraid of?

What about the future scares me? ↓

Card 3

Card 1
Card 2

Card 6

Card 1: Who am I? ↑

How am I afraid? → Card 5

Deconstruction/Application Day 13

1. **Who am I?** **What am I afraid of?**

_____ _____

2. Read cards **1** and **2** as a combination. What about your spiritual essence is influenced or characterized by this fear?

_____

_____

_____

What past life event caused this fear?	Who am I afraid of?
How am I afraid? (triggers)	**What about the future scares me?**

3. On a scale of **1 to 10**, with **10** being *"I've uncovered and identified a recognizable fear,"* and **1** being, *"I have no concrete leads on what my fears might be,"* how connected did you feel to this spread?

1   2   3   4   5   6   7   8   9   10

Day 14: Phobias and Fears Spread 2

Root-Focused

Use this spread to look closely at the cause of your fear or phobia.

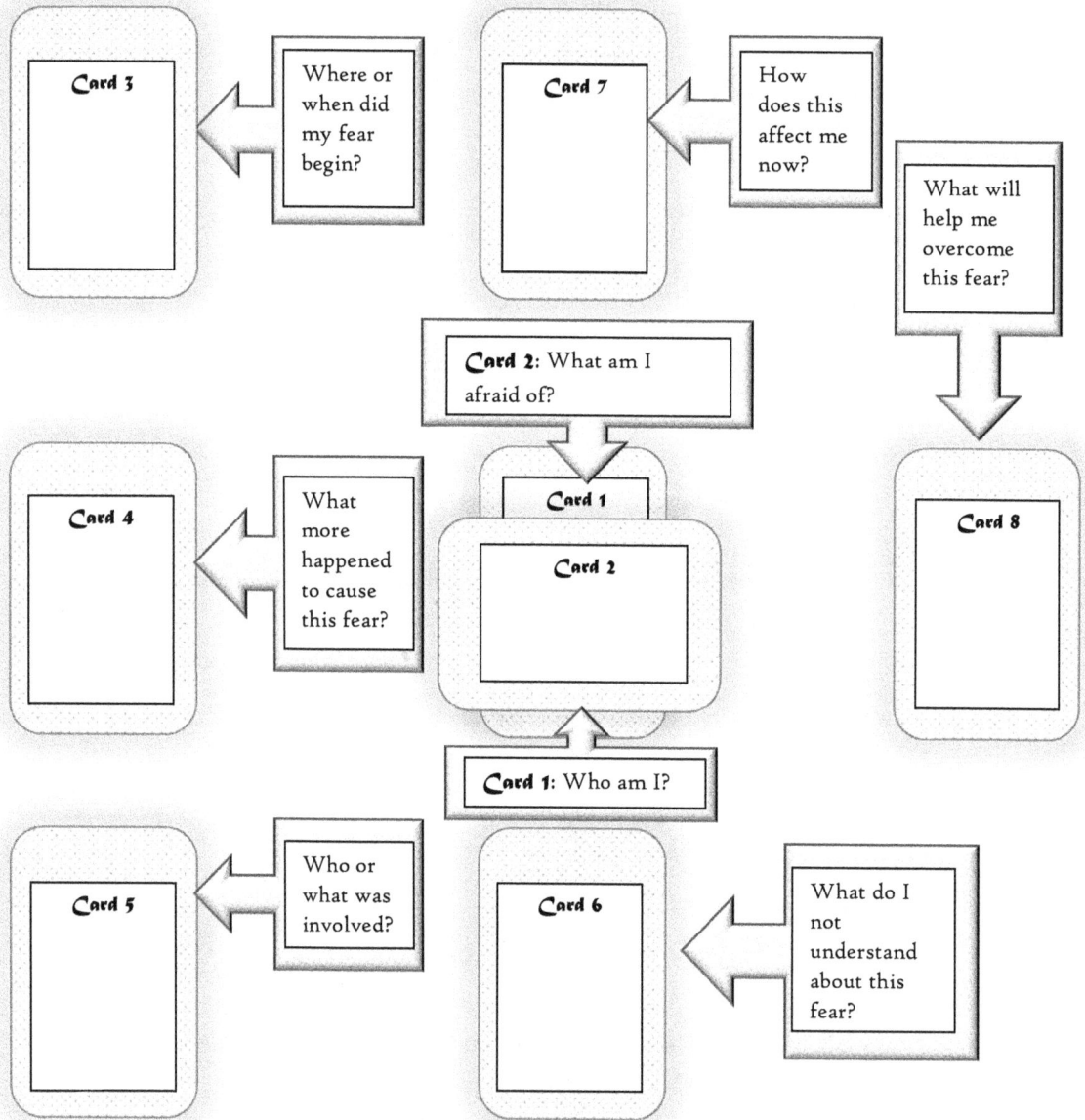

Card 3

Where or when did my fear begin?

Card 7

How does this affect me now?

What will help me overcome this fear?

Card 2: What am I afraid of?

Card 4

What more happened to cause this fear?

Card 1

Card 2

Card 8

Card 1: Who am I?

Card 5

Who or what was involved?

Card 6

What do I not understand about this fear?

Deconstruction/Application Day 14

1. **Who am I?**   **What am I afraid of?**

_____   _____

2. Read cards **1** and **2** as a combination. What about your spiritual essence is influenced or characterized by this fear?

_____
_____
_____

Where or when did this fear begin?	What more happened to cause this fear?
Who or what was involved?	What do I not understand?
How does this affect me now?	How will I overcome this fear?

3. On a scale of **1 to 10**, with **10** being *"I've uncovered and identified a recognizable fear,"* and **1** being, *"I have no concrete leads on what my fears might be,"* how connected did you feel to this spread?

       1   2   3   4   5   6   7   8   9   10

Day 15: Phobias and Fears Spread 3

Healing-Focused

Use this spread to look closely at solutions for overcoming this phobia or fear.

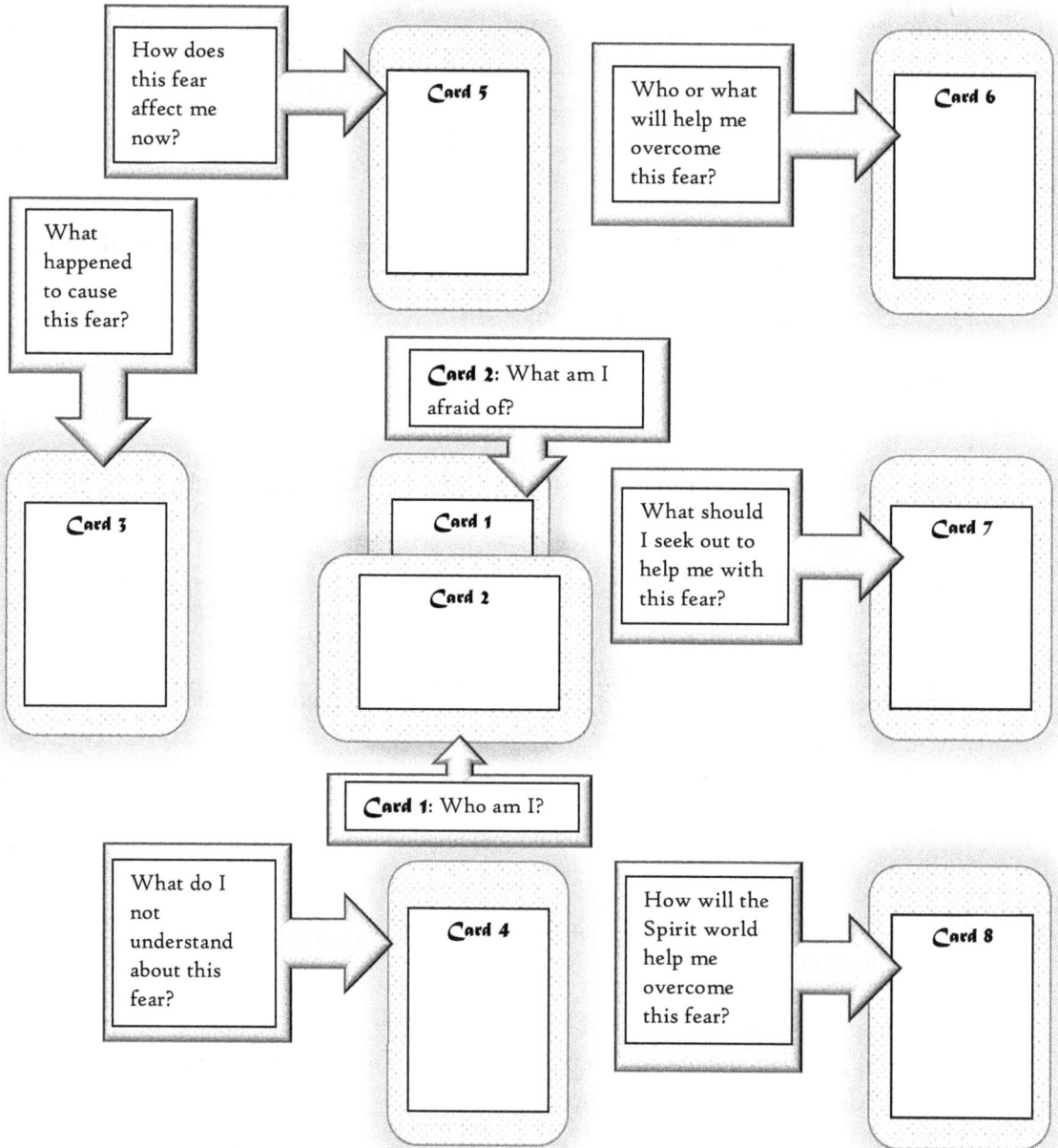

How does this fear affect me now? → Card 5

Who or what will help me overcome this fear? → Card 6

What happened to cause this fear? → Card 3

Card 2: What am I afraid of? → Card 1

Card 2

What should I seek out to help me with this fear? → Card 7

Card 1: Who am I? → Card 2

What do I not understand about this fear? → Card 4

How will the Spirit world help me overcome this fear? → Card 8

Deconstruction/Application Day 15

1. **Who am I?**   **What am I afraid of?**

   _____   _____

2. Read cards **1** and **2** as a combination. What about your spiritual essence is influenced or characterized by this fear?

   _____

   _____

   _____

What happened to cause this fear?	How does this affect me now?
What do I not understand?	Who or what will help me overcome this fear?
What should I seek out to help me with this fear?	How will the spirit world help me overcome this fear?

3. On a scale of **1 to 10**, with **10** being _"I've uncovered and identified a recognizable fear,"_ and **1** being, _"I have no concrete leads on what my fears might be,"_ how connected did you feel to this spread?

   1   2   3   4   5   6   7   8   9   10

Days 16-18: Dreams Spreads

The symbology offered in dreams is limitless. There would need to be another book on dream interpretation alone to do this subject justice (and many books have been written for that purpose). Try to discern whether what you are dreaming was an actual event or a metaphor by paying close attention to your feelings during the dream. If your emotions are highly reactive to what is going on in the dream, it's likely a memory. If your emotional state, thoughts and feelings appear to contradict the events in the dream, then it's likely a metaphor.

Below is a chart for reading each tarot card as a message for interpreting your dream. You can also read the images on your cards as symbols as well.

Spread 1 is designed to connect your dream to your higher consciousness and subconscious. *Spread 2* is designed to help you interpret the advice offered in a dream, and *Spread 3* is designed to help you translate your dream into a message from a Higher Power.

Dream Interpretation Reference Guide

Major Arcana

0-The Fool	You need to start over	11-Strength	You will heal from this wound
1-The Magician	You need to manifest	12- The Hanged man	Unfinished business
2-The High Priestess	You need to observe rather than act	13- Death	Something is over or will be over soon
3-The Empress	You need to create	14- Temperance	You need to find balance
4-The Emperor	You need boundaries	15- The Devil	You need to work on unhealthy fixations and addictions
5-The Hierophant	You either need more or less religious structure in your life	16- The Tower	Lean into the change
6-The Lovers	You need to make an important choice; life junction	17- The Star	You need to understand your path
7-The Chariot	You need to pursue what you desire	18- The Moon	There's something you're not seeing
8- Justice	You should do what is fair	19- The Sun	Joy is on the horizon
9- The Hermit	You need meditation	20- Judgment	A huge spiritual breakthrough is imminent
10- Wheel of Fortune	You can't stop the change coming	21- The World	The world is yours

Cups

Ace of Cups	Love message from the spirit world	Eight of Cups	Walk away from something toxic
Two of Cups	Message about a relationship	Nine of Cups	Wish will be granted
Three of Cups	Message about or delivered through a friend	Ten of Cups	Fulfilling love is coming
Four of Cups	Find your passion	Page of Cups	Someone will help you with your problem
Five of Cups	Focus on what you have	Knight of Cups	Expect an offer
Six of Cups	Look to the past for answers	Queen of Cups	You need love
Seven of Cups	Focus on your desires	King of Cups	A period of emotional stability is before you

Swords

Ace of Swords	The truth is coming forth within you	Eight of Swords	You will figure a way out of this problem
Two of Swords	Identify your blind spot	Nine of Swords	Past life information in dream
Three of Swords	Nurse your broken heart	Ten of Swords	The worst is over
Four of Swords	You need a retreat	Page of Swords	Prepare carefully for the future
Five of Swords	Watch out for an abusive person	Knight of Swords	Prepare to battle
Six of Swords	You need to move or take a trip	Queen of Swords	Articulate what you need
Seven of Swords	Someone is betraying you	King of Swords	Consider your problem logically

Wands

Ace of Wands	Fertile (literally or metaphorically)	Eight of Wands	Important news coming
Two of Wands	You need to set goals	Nine of Wands	You will figure out how to get un-stuck
Three of Wands	You need to act on your goals	Ten of Wands	You have too many burdens right now
Four of Wands	You are entering a period of stability	Page of Wands	A messenger will appear
Five of Wands	Someone wants to compete with you	Knight of Wands	You have incredible drive right now
Six of Wands	Victory is imminent	Queen of Wands	You can charm your way out of this problem
Seven of Wands	Prepare to defend yourself	King of Wands	Use your charisma

Pentacles

Ace of Pentacles	Money is coming in	Eight of Pentacles	Enter school or an internship
Two of Pentacles	Consider changing something	Nine of Pentacles	Don't be afraid to do this alone
Three of Pentacles	Work as a team	Ten of Pentacles	Take something off your plate
Four of Pentacles	Save money for now	Page of Pentacles	Important project coming up
Five of Pentacles	Don't lose hope during this time	Knight of Pentacles	Stay where you are for now
Six of Pentacles	Someone will help you	Queen of Pentacles	Nurture others
Seven of Pentacles	You'll have to wait for results	King of Pentacles	Provide for others

Day 16: Dreams Spread 1 Consciousness Spread

Use a selected dream from your dream journal. Reflect on these three levels of consciousness in order to interpret the dream's deeper messages.

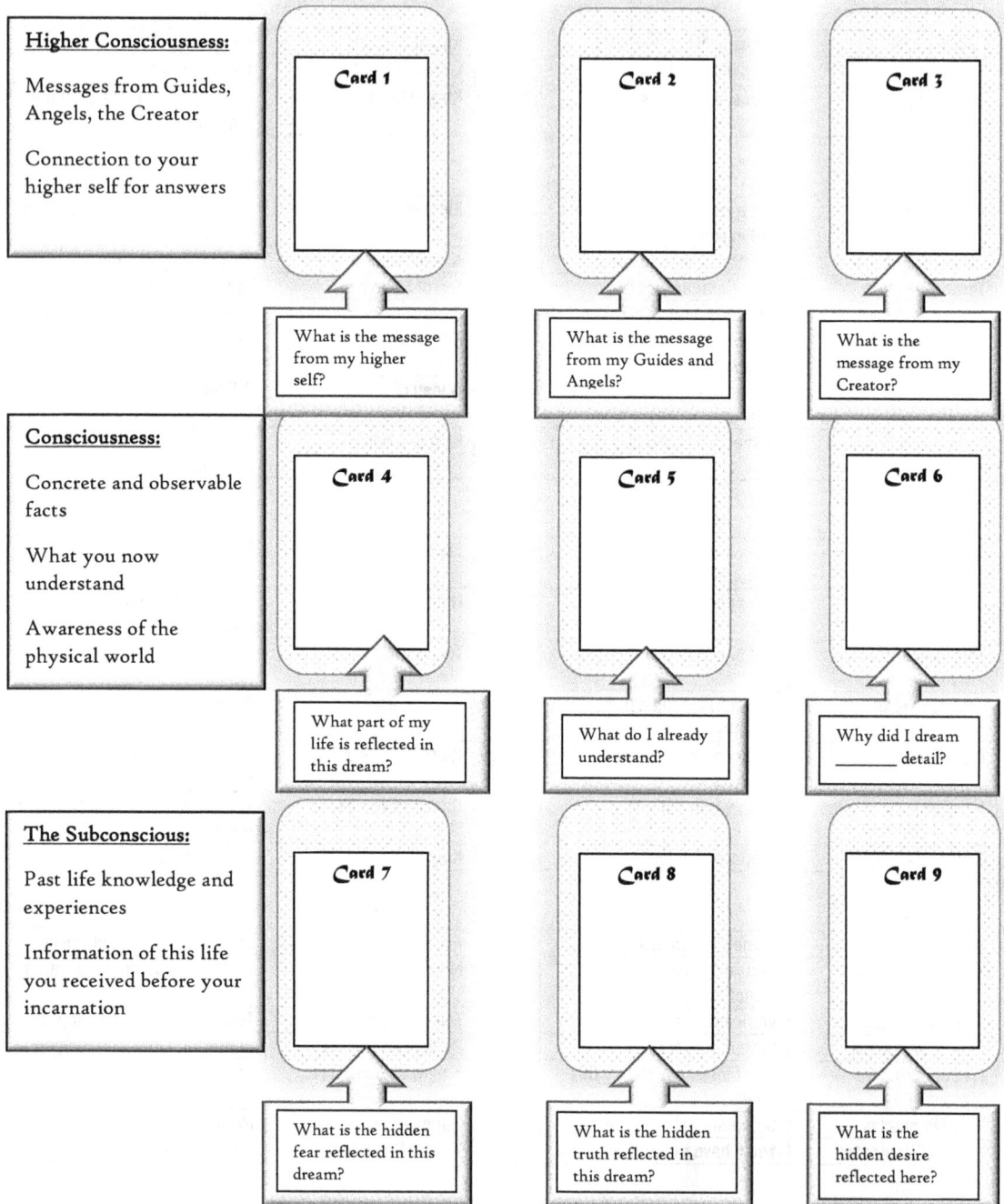

Higher Consciousness:

Messages from Guides, Angels, the Creator

Connection to your higher self for answers

Card 1

Card 2

Card 3

What is the message from my higher self?

What is the message from my Guides and Angels?

What is the message from my Creator?

Consciousness:

Concrete and observable facts

What you now understand

Awareness of the physical world

Card 4

Card 5

Card 6

What part of my life is reflected in this dream?

What do I already understand?

Why did I dream _____ detail?

The Subconscious:

Past life knowledge and experiences

Information of this life you received before your incarnation

Card 7

Card 8

Card 9

What is the hidden fear reflected in this dream?

What is the hidden truth reflected in this dream?

What is the hidden desire reflected here?

Deconstruction/Application Day 16

Higher Consciousness	What is the message from my higher self?	What is the message from my guides and angels?	What is the message from my creator?
Consciousness	What part of my life is reflected in this dream?	What do I already understand?	Why did I dream _____? (insert your specific detail (s)
The Subconscious	What is the hidden fear reflected in this dream?	What is the hidden truth reflected in this dream?	What is the hidden desire reflected here?

On a scale of **1 to 10**, with **10** being *"I fully understand the spiritual message behind this dream,"* and **1** being, *"I can make no spiritual connection to this dream,"* how connected did you feel to this spread?

1   2   3   4   5   6   7   8   9   10

Day 17: Dreams Spread 2 Advice Spread

Use this spread to interpret a dream as advice.

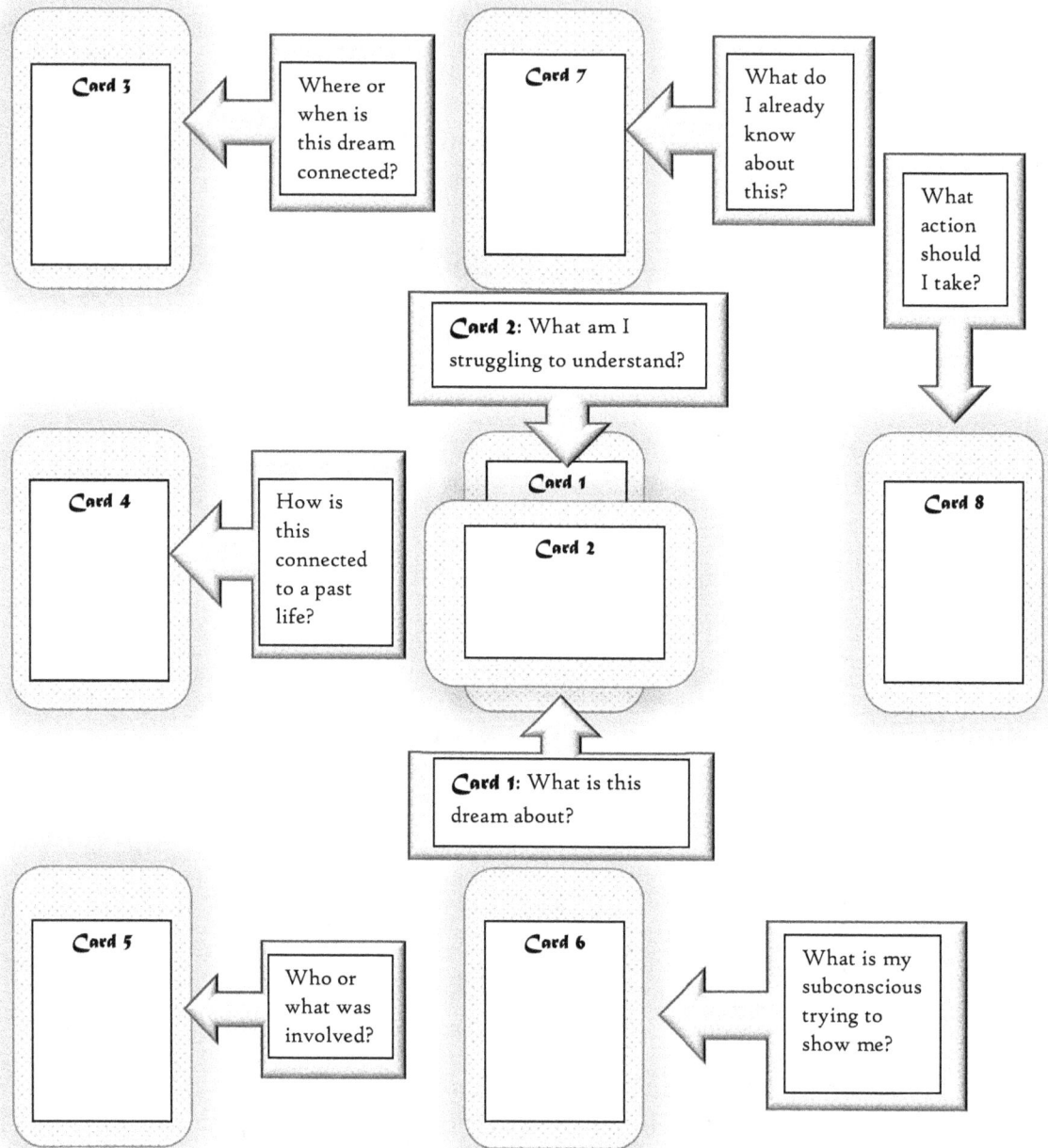

Card 3

Where or when is this dream connected?

Card 7

What do I already know about this?

What action should I take?

Card 2: What am I struggling to understand?

Card 1

Card 2

Card 4

How is this connected to a past life?

Card 8

Card 1: What is this dream about?

Card 5

Who or what was involved?

Card 6

What is my subconscious trying to show me?

Deconstruction/Application Day 17

1. What is the dream about?   What am I struggling to understand?

_____   _____

2. Read cards **1** and **2** as a combination. What message do they offer when read together?

_____

_____

_____

Where or when is this dream connected?	How is this connected to a past life?
Who or what was involved?	What do I already know about this issue?
What is my subconscious trying to show me?	What action should I take?

3. On a scale of **1 to 10**, with **10** being _"I fully understand the spiritual message behind this dream,"_ and **1** being, _"I can make no spiritual connection to this dream,"_ how connected did you feel to this spread?

        1   2   3   4   5   6   7   8   9   10

Day 18: Dreams Spread 3

Decoding the Message

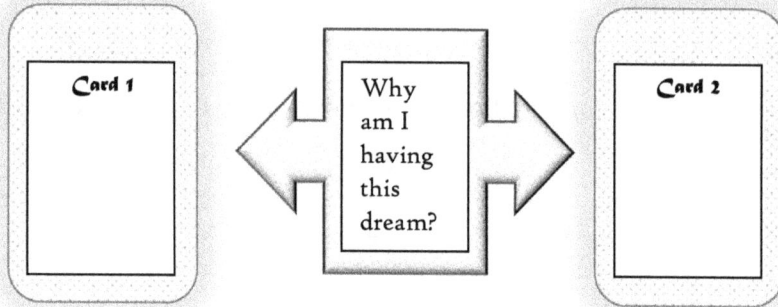

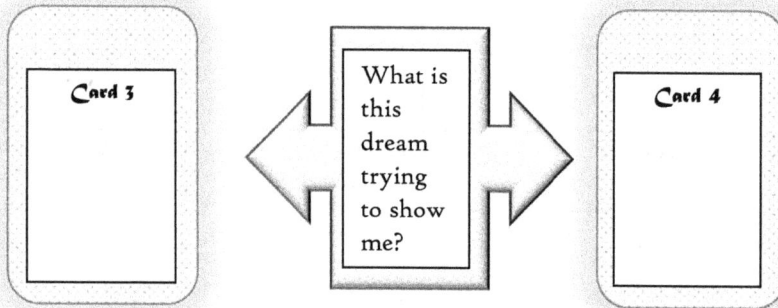

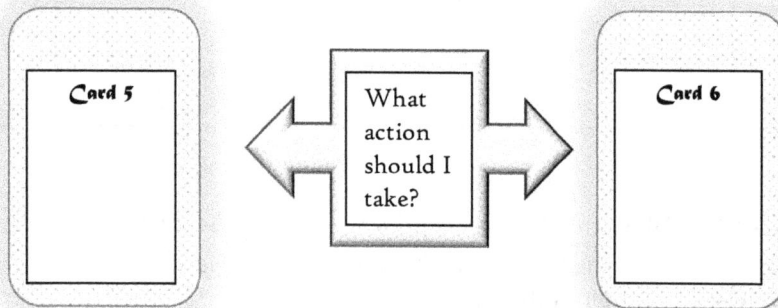

Card 1	Why am I having this dream?	Card 2

Card 3	What is this dream trying to show me?	Card 4

Card 5	What action should I take?	Card 6

Deconstruction/Application Day 18

Why am I having this dream? **Card 1**	Why am I having this dream? **Card 2**
Draw an interpretation to this question by reading these two cards in combination:	

What is this dream trying to show me? **Card 3**	What is this dream trying to show me? **Card 4**
Draw an interpretation to this question by reading these two cards in combination:	

What action should I take? **Card 5**	What action should I take? **Card 6**
Draw an interpretation to this question by reading these two cards in combination:	

On a scale of **1 to 10**, with **10** being *"I fully understand the spiritual message behind this dream,"* and **1** being, *"I can make no spiritual connection to this dream,"* how connected did you feel to this spread?

1   2   3   4   5   6   7   8   9   10

Days 19-21: Life Goals Spreads

How many life goals do you have? Some have several whereas others may have only one. A life goal is a specific achievement you are hoping to accomplish during your time here. It is designed based on your previous lifetimes, according to how you failed and what you desired and desire now. We are all working to become kind, thoughtful, loving, talented and skilled masters of ourselves. The specifics on how you accomplish that ideal is found in your life goals.

Spread 1 will help you to identify a goal. Repeat this spread either until you found something that resonates through your being, or until you have enough repeating cards that you can't deny the message. Then move on to *Spread 2* to help understand why you have a particular goal.

Spread 3 is designed to widen the lens: what did you achieve before, and what will the new goal be in your next lifetime? Taking a wide-scope look at your progression can help orient you toward accomplishing your goal in this life.

Life Goals Reference Guide

Major Arcana

0-The Fool	To have a totally new life experience		11-Strength	To heal self and others
1-The Magician	To learn how to manifest in the world		12- The Hanged man	To endure life without giving up
2-The High Priestess	To learn how to develop your intuition		13- Death	To communicate with the spirit world
3-The Empress	To give birth to either children or art (or both)		14- Temperance	To find balance, harmony and healthy routine
4-The Emperor	To provide structure in the world		15- The Devil	To conquer addiction and/or obsessions/therapist
5-The Hierophant	To belong to a faith community		16- The Tower	To change the social structure of the world
6-The Lovers	To make the right life choices		17- The Star	To remind others of our spiritual home
7-The Chariot	To set worldly goals and achieve them		18- The Moon	To share your intuitive gifts
8- Justice	To bring justice to the world		19- The Sun	To spread joy
9- The Hermit	To become a teacher		20- Judgment	To help self and others gain clarity
10- Wheel of Fortune	To ride the waves of life in peace		21- The World	To heal and protect the environment

Cups

Ace of Cups	To spread love in the world		Eight of Cups	To make difficult changes
Two of Cups	To give and receive love		Nine of Cups	To receive (or grant) a wish
Three of Cups	To love and entertain those in your circle		Ten of Cups	To find emotional fulfillment
Four of Cups	To develop a passion		Page of Cups	To offer help to others
Five of Cups	To achieve or acquire something you were denied before		Knight of Cups	To rescue others
Six of Cups	To do past life work		Queen of Cups	To care for the sick
Seven of Cups	To chase your wildest dreams		King of Cups	To demonstrate goodness to others

Swords

Ace of Swords	To tell the truth/writing		Eight of Swords	To live a life of incredible struggle
Two of Swords	To gain perspective through a vastly different life		Nine of Swords	To conquer your mind
Three of Swords	To heal the broken hearted		Ten of Swords	To lose everything, then gain it back
Four of Swords	To comfort the grieving		Page of Swords	To prepare for your next life
Five of Swords	To support and aid those who have experienced abuse		Knight of Swords	To fight on behalf of others
Six of Swords	To travel the world		Queen of Swords	To leave a legacy through writing
Seven of Swords	To develop successful strategies		King of Swords	To leave a legacy through science

Wands

Ace of Wands	To honor your creativity		Eight of Wands	To advance technology
Two of Wands	To build good karma		Nine of Wands	To absolve a spiritual blockage
Three of Wands	To receive good karma		Ten of Wands	To manage depression
Four of Wands	To enjoy stability		Page of Wands	To inspire others
Five of Wands	To compete for greatness		Knight of Wands	To chase your dreams
Six of Wands	Great lifetime achievement		Queen of Wands	To create aesthetic beauty
Seven of Wands	To establish boundaries with others		King of Wands	To lead others

Pentacles

Ace of Pentacles	To have abundance in the material world		Eight of Pentacles	To gain higher education
Two of Pentacles	To perform		Nine of Pentacles	To gain independence
Three of Pentacles	To develop teamwork		Ten of Pentacles	To demonstrate strength to others
Four of Pentacles	To acquire savings for posterity		Page of Pentacles	To work on a project
Five of Pentacles	To develop self-worth		Knight of Pentacles	To demonstrate stability to others
Six of Pentacles	To provide for others' needs		Queen of Pentacles	To nurture others
Seven of Pentacles	To develop patience		King of Pentacles	To provide for others

Day 19: Life Goals Spread 1

Identifying Your Goal(s)

You probably have more than one life goal. These spreads focus on one goal at time, so it might be helpful to do the spreads more than once. Select cards that represent your goal for spreads 2 and 3 once you have clarity about what your goals are.

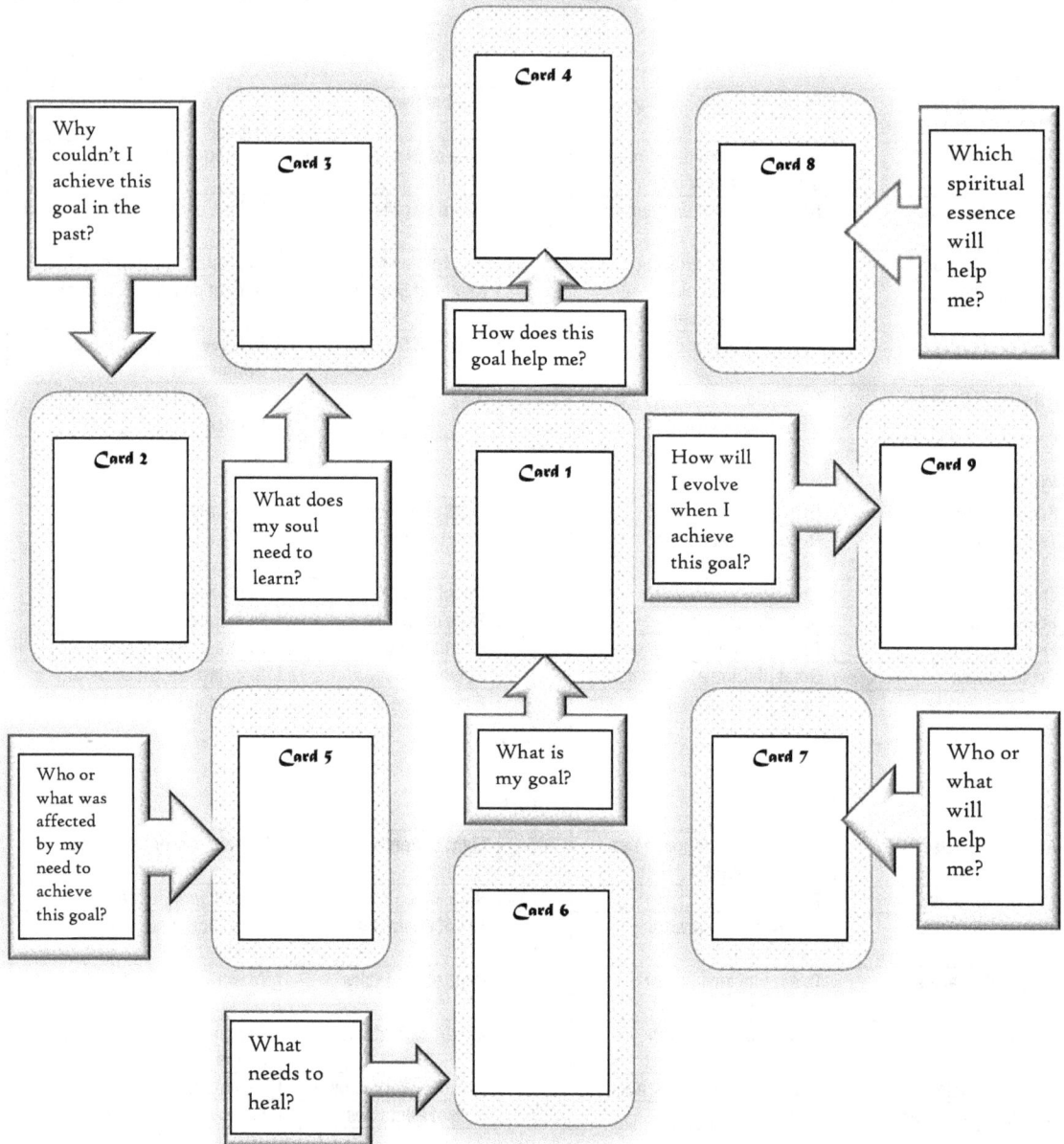

Card 4

Why couldn't I achieve this goal in the past?

Card 3

Card 8

Which spiritual essence will help me?

How does this goal help me?

Card 2

What does my soul need to learn?

Card 1

How will I evolve when I achieve this goal?

Card 9

Who or what was affected by my need to achieve this goal?

Card 5

What is my goal?

Card 7

Who or what will help me?

Card 6

What needs to heal?

Deconstruction/Application Day 19

1. **What is my goal?**

_____

The Past	The Present/Future
Why couldn't I achieve this goal in the past?	How does this goal help me?
What does my soul need to learn?	Which spiritual essence will help me?
Who or what was affected by my need to achieve this goal?	Who or what will help me?
What still needs to heal?	How will I evolve when I achieve this goal?

2. On a scale of **1 to 10**, with **10** being "*I have a clear vision of my lifetime's goals and how I will achieve them*," and **1** being, "*I have no clarification about my lifetime's goals*," how connected did you feel to this spread?

1   2   3   4   5   6   7   8   9   10

Day 20: Life Goals Spread 2

Understanding Why

For this spread, you will look at the energetic impacts of your goal, both past and future.

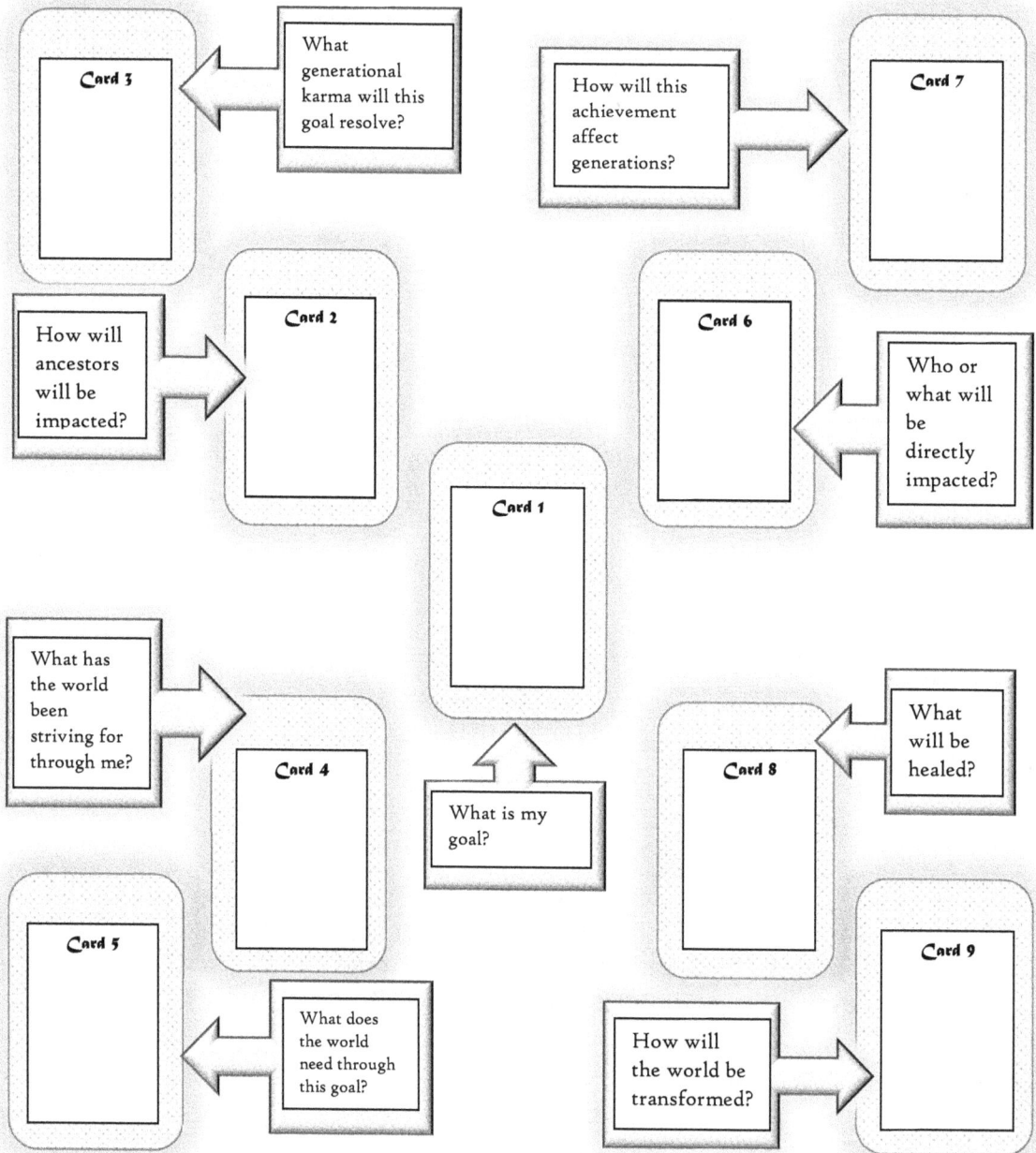

Card 3 — What generational karma will this goal resolve?

Card 7 ← How will this achievement affect generations?

Card 2 ← How will ancestors will be impacted?

Card 6 — Who or what will be directly impacted?

Card 1

Card 4 ← What has the world been striving for through me?

Card 1 — What is my goal?

Card 8 ← What will be healed?

Card 5 — What does the world need through this goal?

Card 9 ← How will the world be transformed?

Deconstruction/Application Day 20

1.   **What is my goal?**

How my goal will affect past karma	How my goal will affect the future
What generational karma will be resolved?	How will this achievement affect future generations?
How will my ancestors will be impacted?	Who or what will be impacted in the future?
What has the world been striving for through me?	What will be healed
What has the world needed through me?	How will the world be transformed?

2. On a scale of **1 to 10**, with **10** being "*I have a clear vision of my lifetime's goals and how I will achieve them,*" and **1** being, "*I have no clarification about my lifetime's goals,*" how connected did you feel to this spread?

1   2   3   4   5   6   7   8   9   10

Day 21: Life Goals Spread 3

Progression of the Soul

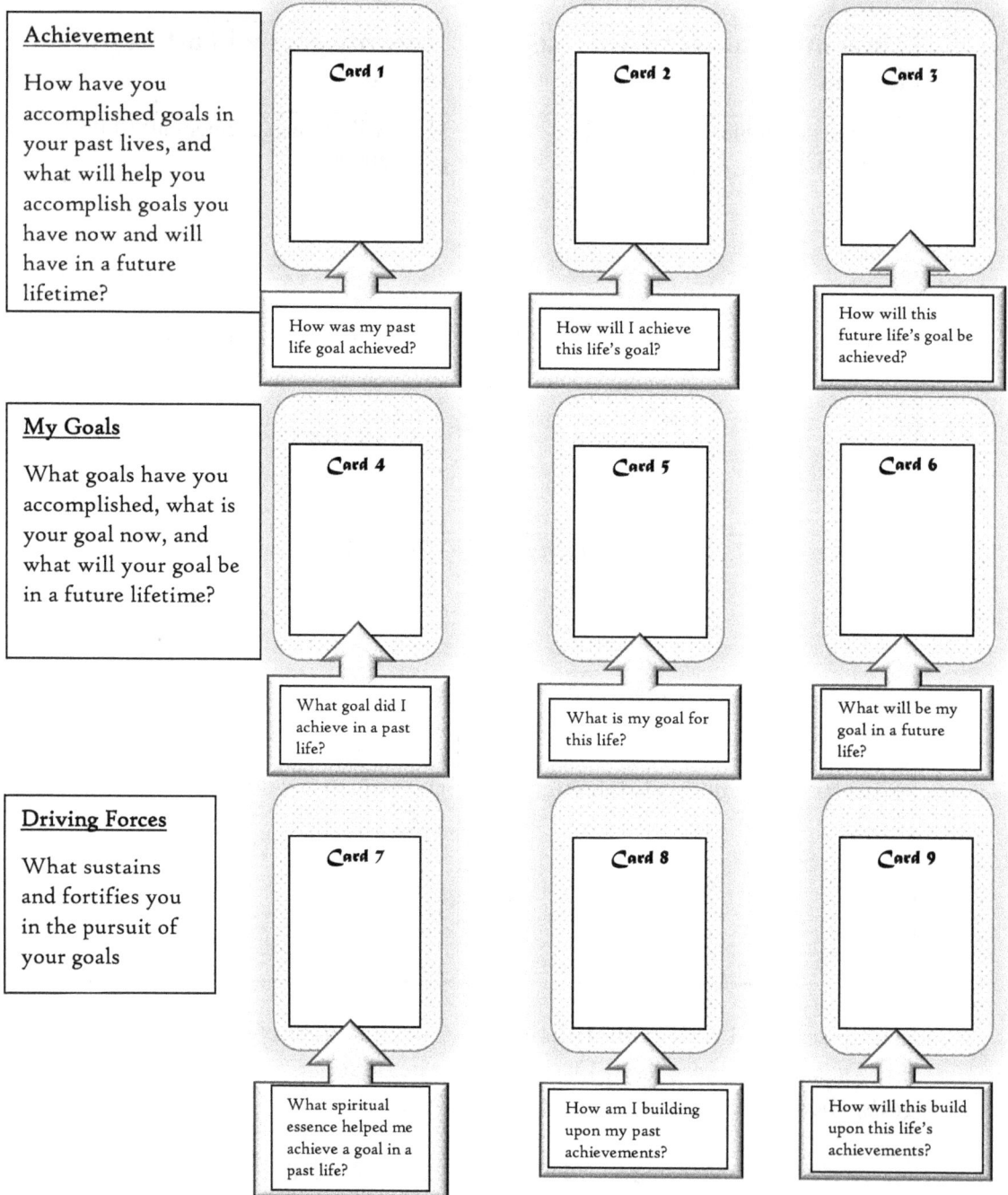

Achievement

How have you accomplished goals in your past lives, and what will help you accomplish goals you have now and will have in a future lifetime?

Card 1

How was my past life goal achieved?

Card 2

How will I achieve this life's goal?

Card 3

How will this future life's goal be achieved?

My Goals

What goals have you accomplished, what is your goal now, and what will your goal be in a future lifetime?

Card 4

What goal did I achieve in a past life?

Card 5

What is my goal for this life?

Card 6

What will be my goal in a future life?

Driving Forces

What sustains and fortifies you in the pursuit of your goals

Card 7

What spiritual essence helped me achieve a goal in a past life?

Card 8

How am I building upon my past achievements?

Card 9

How will this build upon this life's achievements?

Deconstruction/Application Day 21

Achievements	How was my past life goal achieved?	How will I achieve this life's goal?	How will this future life's goal be achieved?
My Goals	What goal did I achieve in a past life?	What is my goal for this life?	What will be my goal in a future life?
Driving Forces	What spiritual essence helped me achieve a goal in a past life?	How am I building upon my past achievements?	How will this build upon this life's achievements?

On a scale of **1 to 10**, with **10** being "*I have a clear vision of my lifetime's goals and how I will achieve them*," and **1** being, "*I have no clarification about my lifetime's goals*," how connected did you feel to this spread?

1   2   3   4   5   6   7   8   9   10

Post-Assessment and Reflection

CONGRATULATIONS for making it through all 21 days of spreads! I expect there were frustrating and confusing moments, as well as some spiritual and remarkable moments. We are now going to complete a few tasks that should help you reflect on how much you've grown and learned over the course.

First, we are going to repeat the assessment you did before you started the coursework.

Pull two cards, both with the question: *Who was I?*

Write the name of the card on each in the diagram below.

Card 1

Card 2

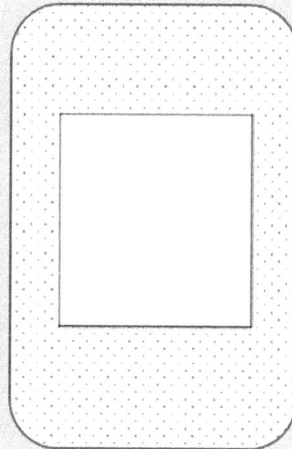

1. Visual/Spiritual

For each of the cards, connect the images to your emotions. What do you feel when you look at this card? Forget, momentarily, what you know about the meaning of the cards or the words printed on them. Stay grounded in emotion/feelings, and what the image encourages you to feel, and not in ideas or language. Emotions are the language of Spirit, so you are most likely to make a connection and receive a message here, in this space.

A.) What did you feel while looking at the image on Card 1?

_____

_____

_____

B.) What did you feel while looking at the image on Card 2?

_____

_____

_____

After each reading, I want you to do a self-assessment to gauge your comfort level and success with this process.

C.) On a scale of **1 to 10**, with **10** being *"I was overcome with emotion and nearly brought to tears"* and **1** being *"I must be Vulcan,"* how emotional did you feel looking at the image on **Card 1**?

1   2   3   4   5   6   7   8   9   10

D.) On a scale of **1 to 10**, with **10** being *"I was overcome with emotion and nearly brought to tears"* and **1** being *"I must be Vulcan,"* how emotional did you feel looking at the image on **Card 2**?

1   2   3   4   5   6   7   8   9   10

E.) On a scale of **1 to 10**, with **10** being *"I felt God/Goddess/Universe speaking directly to me through the card"* and **1** being *"This is only cardboard,"* how much of a spiritual connection did you feel gazing at the image on **Card 1**?

1   2   3   4   5   6   7   8   9   10

F.) On a scale of **1 to 10**, with **10** being *"I felt God/Goddess/Universe speaking directly to me through the card"* and **1** being *"This is only cardboard,"* how much of a spiritual connection did you feel gazing at the image on **Card 2**?

   1 2 3 4 5 6 7 8 9 10

2. Language

Now you're going to focus on language in your response to the cards. You can examine what the language printed on the cards means outside of a tarot/oracle context, or you can focus on the language that is commonly associated with that card (this exercise will look vastly different depending on if you have experience with tarot or not).

 A.) What are all the word/language associations you have with **Card 1**?

  _____

  _____

 B.) What are all the word/language associations you have with **Card 2**?

  _____

  _____

I'd like you to build upon your existing knowledge of this language. Now, we are going to narrow the scope and shift away from every word association we might have, and instead focus on tarot/oracle interpretations. Get out the book that came with your deck, and pull out at least two more resources. These can be other books you have on hand, or websites. Research each of your cards and compare/contrast information between sources.

 C.) What new language can you identify for **Card 1**?

  _____

  _____

  _____

D.) What new language can you identify for **Card 2**?

_____

_____

_____

Next, let's make a comparison of all your language associations to your emotional response.

E.) When you compare your language associations to your emotional response for **Card 1**, how well do they align, if at all?

_____

_____

F.) When you compare your language associations to your emotional response for **Card 2**, how well do they align, if at all?

_____

_____

G.) On a scale of **1 to 10** with **10** being, "*My emotional response and language associations were completely in alignment*" to "*Neither card seemed to connect my emotional response to its intended meaning,*" how well do you feel your spiritual and intellectual response to these two cards aligned?

1   **2**   **3**   **4**   **5**   **6**   **7**   **8**   **9**   **10**

3. Deconstruction and Application

Now that you have explored each card emotionally and intellectually, the third step is to apply that information to yourself in an interpretive way. Deconstruction is a term that means breaking down parts. Here, we break down the emotional and intellectual aspects of a card and then apply them in a personal and interpretive way.

Reflect over your responses to E and F on the previous page. With that information, we are going to apply it to our question: *Who was I?* This process involves evaluating the different aspects of the card, and then reconstructing those responses to apply to a potential identity (potential identity because that is the question we asked). Certain aspects of each card from the visual and language exercises will now come to the forefront, and certain aspects will now fade to the background or be eliminated entirely if they don't apply, if they contradict, or if they don't resonate with you.

Again, revisit your emotions during this process and rely on your intuition to tell you where the focus should go. Although I probably wouldn't deviate entirely from a card's intended energy, it's okay to reinterpret a card based on the image or where you feel your intuition is pulling you. What's important is that you understand to what extent you are deviating from the logical aspects of that card, so that you may do it with intention and clarity.

A.) Now, answer the question: *Who was I?*

Card 1:

_____

_____

Card 2:

_____

_____

B.) On a scale of **1 to 10**, with **10** being "I understood the deconstruction process perfectly and was able to apply this process with ease" and **1** being, "I feel I don't understand the deconstruction process," how comfortable were you with this last step?

1   2   3   4   5   6   7   8   9   10

C.) On a scale of **1 to 10** with **10** being, "I feel I was able to connect to and interpret these cards for myself" and **1** being, "I feel a total disconnection to the intuitive process," how connected to Spirit did you feel during the reading?

1   2   3   4   5   6   7   8   9   10

We are now going to compare your assessment scores.

Item	Pre-Assessment	Post-Assessment	Difference -/+	Improvement? (yes/no)
Visual C				
Visual D				
Visual E				
Visual F				
Language G				
Application B				
Application C				

In review of the above information, in what ways does it appear you have grown?

_____

_____

_____

_____

_____

_____

In review of the above information, in what ways does it appear you have not grown?

_____

_____

_____

_____

_____

_____

Look through this workbook, and make a ranking of your top three spreads, those spreads that you rated the highest in connection:

1:_____

2:_____

3:_____

What do you believe you'll always remember about these spreads? What stands out to you? What do you think of first?

_____
_____
_____
_____
_____
_____
_____
_____
_____
_____
_____
_____
_____
_____
_____
_____
_____

This concludes the 21-day course! Thank you so much for trusting me to guide you through this journey. Your past lives echo through your essence and influence your interactions in the world in this life. Through contemplative explorations, you can work to break barriers and evolve in the ways your soul deeply desires. Your journey is unique and powerful and worth the energetic investment you have put into this spiritual navigation.

I have included a repetition of the workbook pages if you want to repeat some of these spreads. This can be a valuable journal to keep as your life progresses! Please stop by and leave a review at redorchidpublishing.com or on amazon.com if you felt this journey was worth the cost and effort!

Happy Divining!

Melanny Eva Henson

Day 1: Spiritual Essence Spread 1

4- Draw three cards that represent three different qualities of your spiritual essence for cards 1-3.
5- Draw one card that represents how all these qualities impact your life.
6- Draw one card that represents how these qualities might make you vulnerable

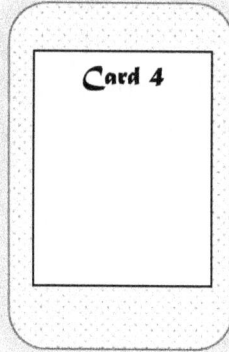

Card 4

What impact do these qualities have on this life?

Card 2

Card 1

Card 3

Spiritual Essence

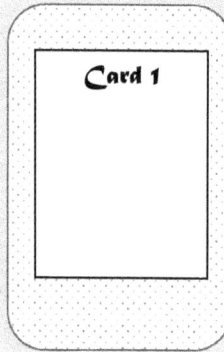

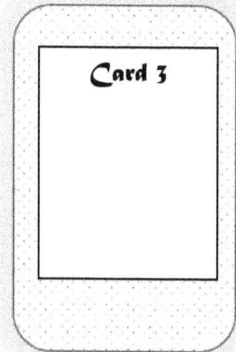

Spiritual Essence

Spiritual Essence

Card 5

What about these qualities makes me vulnerable?

Note: All three cards probably won't connect to both 4 and 5, so follow interpretations that make the most sense, or where you feel pulled

Deconstruction/Application Day 1

1. Record your interpretations for each of the cards:

   Card 1:

   _____

   _____

   Card 2:

   _____

   _____

   Card 3:

   _____

   _____

   Card 4: *What impact do these qualities have?*

   _____

   _____

   Card 5: *What about these qualities makes me vulnerable?*

   _____

   _____

   What is the greatest insight you gained from this spread?

   _____

   _____

   _____

2. On a scale of **1 to 10**, with **10** being *"I definitely felt connected to my spiritual essence,"* and **1** being, *"I'm not sure I had any connection to my spiritual essence,"* how connected did you feel to this spread?

   1   2   3   4   5   6   7   8   9   10

Day 2: Spiritual Essence Spread 2

Pull one card for spiritual essence. Stay in the energy of that essence card and ask, how did this affect me in a past life? Then ask, how does this affect me now? Repeat twice more. Keep cards face down until the spread is complete.

Card 5	Card 2	Card 8
Past Life	Past Life	Past Life
Card 4	Card 1	Card 7
Essence	Essence	Essence
Card 6	Card 3	Card 9
This life	This life	This life

Deconstruction/Application Day 2

	Card 1	Card 4	Card 7
My essence			
How this is connected to the past			
How it is connected to my life now			
Reflection/ Thoughts			

2. What is the greatest insight you gained from this spread?

_____

_____

_____

3. On a scale of **1 to 10**, with **10** being *"I definitely felt connected to my spiritual essence,"* and 1 being, *"I'm not sure I had any connection to my spiritual essence,"* how connected did you feel to this spread?

       1   2   3   4   5   6   7   8   9   10

Day 3: Spiritual Essence Spread 3

For this spread, pick one essence card from Spreads 1 or 2, and pull that from the deck to place in the center of the spread. Choose one that either resonated with you strongly, or one you still have some probing questions about. For the second card, ask where you want to go in this life. We are going to dig deeper on how this essence functions for you. For the question, *Where do I want to go*, this could be applied broadly to mean a destination, personal goal, or spiritual development.

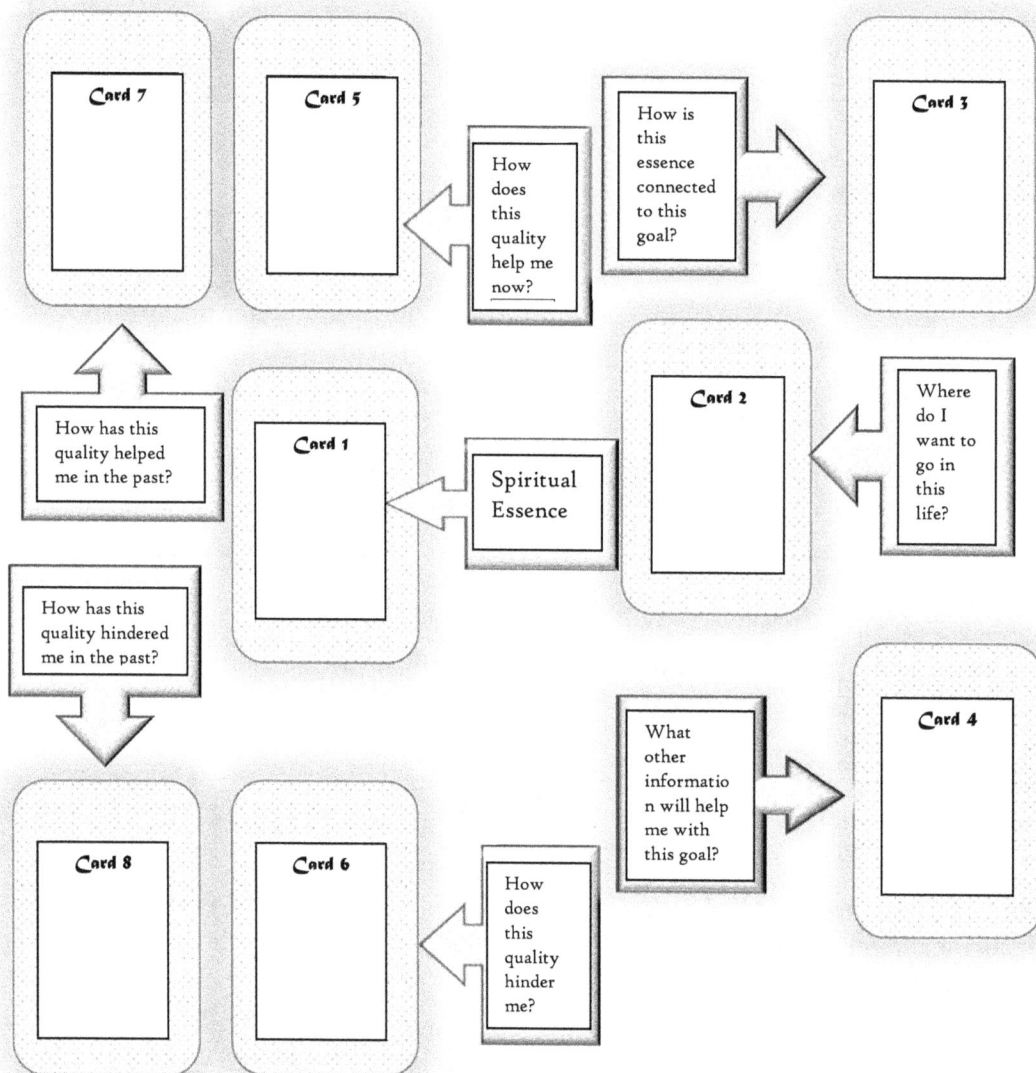

Card 7	Card 5	How does this quality help me now?	How is this essence connected to this goal?	Card 3

How has this quality helped me in the past?	Card 1	Spiritual Essence	Card 2	Where do I want to go in this life?

How has this quality hindered me in the past?

Card 8	Card 6	How does this quality hinder me?	What other information will help me with this goal?	Card 4

Deconstruction/Application Day 3

1.   **The Essence**   **The Goal**

_____   _____

2. Combine **5** and **7**: **How** does this quality help me?

_____

_____

3. Combine **6** and **8**: **How** does this quality hinder me?

_____

_____

4. **What** is the <u>connection</u> between your **essence** and your **goal**?

_____

_____

5. **What** further information do you have about your **goal**? (Card 4)

_____

_____

6. What is the greatest insight you gained from this spread?

_____

_____

_____

7. On a scale of **1 to 10**, with **10** being "*I definitely felt connected to my spiritual essence,*" and **1** being, "*I'm not sure I had any connection to my spiritual essence,*" how connected did you feel to this spread?

   1   2   3   4   5   6   7   8   9   10

Day 4: Narrative Spread 1

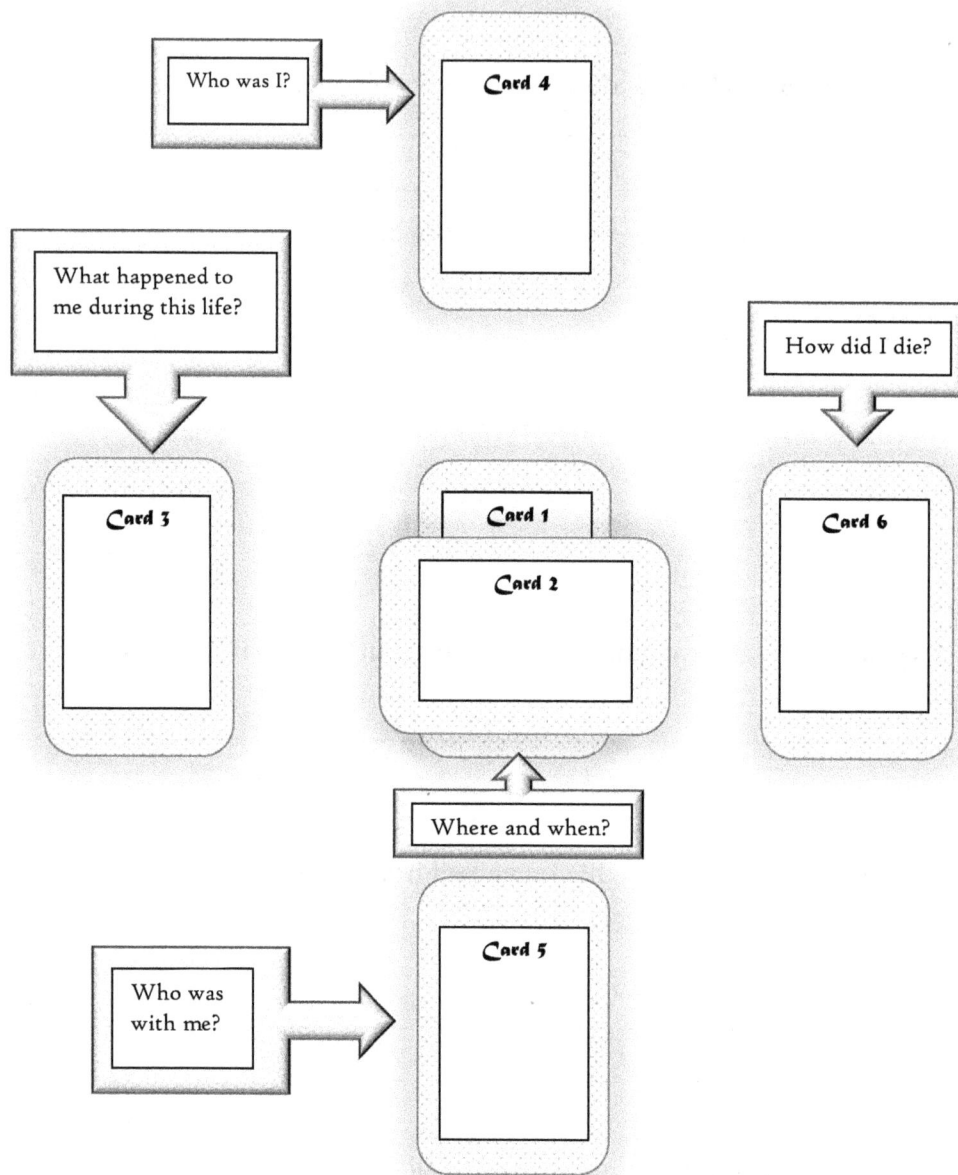

Who was I? → **Card 4**

What happened to me during this life? ↓ **Card 3**

How did I die? ↓ **Card 6**

Card 1

Card 2

Where and when? ↑

Who was with me? → **Card 5**

Deconstruction/Application Day 4

1. **Where**   **When**

_____   _____

Note: You can use cards **1** and **2** interchangeably for place and time. Feel free to use surrounding cards for place and time as well if it makes more sense. If you are using a regular tarot deck, instead ask, *"What was going on in history during this time?"*

To construct a narrative from the cards, you may need to deviate from some of the placements if it makes more sense to do so, (for example: reading Card **3** as a place card rather than what happened). Lean heavily on images and your instinct during this process. Answer the following questions to the best of your ability. Some questions may be inconclusive.

2. **What** happened to me during this life?

_____

_____

3. **Who** was I?

_____

4. **Who** was with me? (**Note**: if you pull "brother" then a brother you have now was with you then).

_____

5. **How** did I die?

_____

6. On a scale of **1 to 10**, with **10** being *"This was a fully formed narrative that resonated with me completely,"* and **1** being, *"I was not able to construct a narrative from this spread,"* how connected did you feel to this spread?

     1   2   3   4   5   6   7   8   9   10

Day 5: Narrative Spread 2

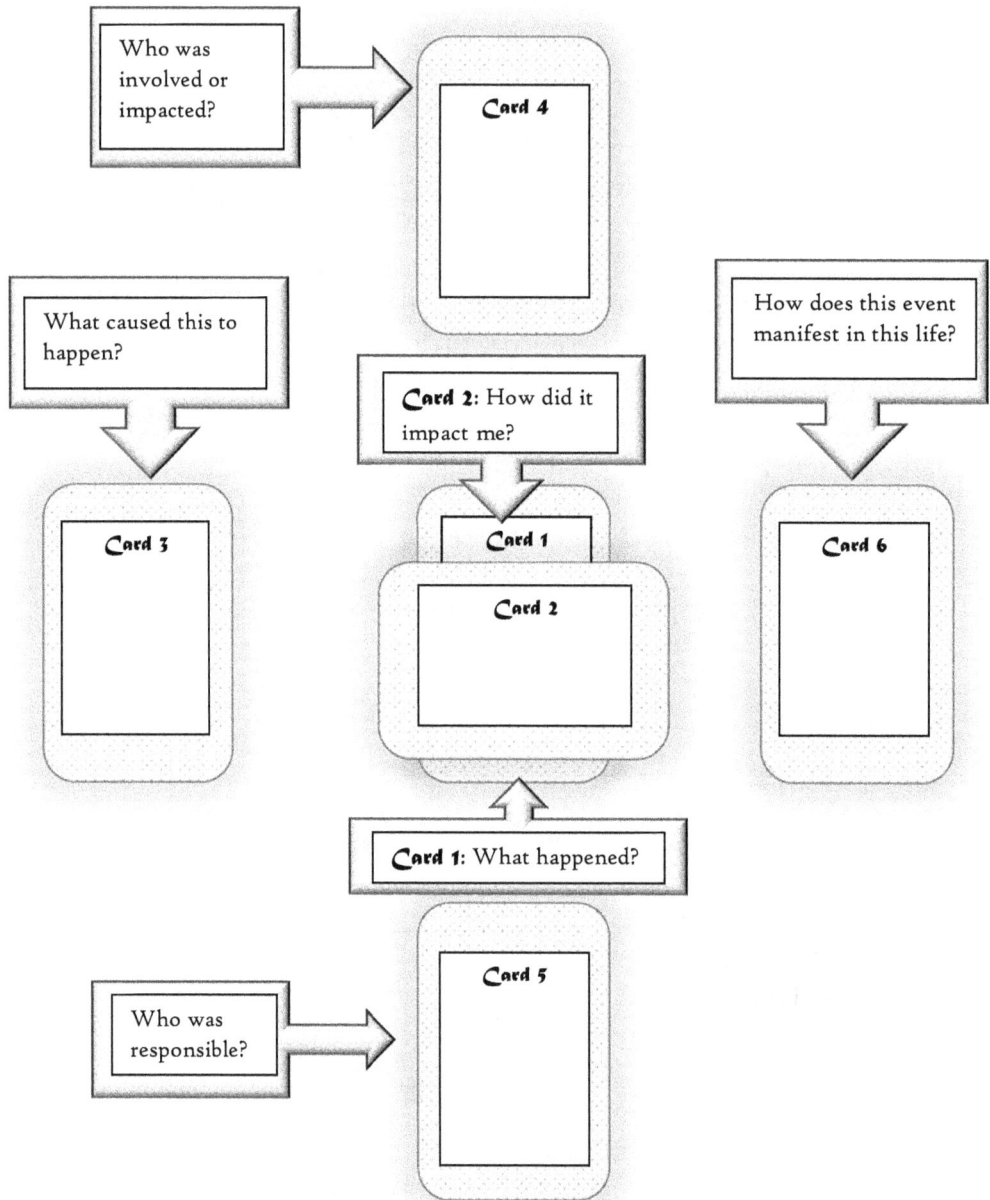

Who was involved or impacted?

Card 4

What caused this to happen?

How does this event manifest in this life?

Card 2: How did it impact me?

Card 3

Card 1

Card 2

Card 6

Card 1: What happened?

Who was responsible?

Card 5

Deconstruction/Application Day 5

1.   **What happened**   **How it impacted me**

_____   _____

To construct a narrative from the cards, you may need to deviate from some of the placements if it makes more sense to do so. Lean heavily on images and your instinct during this process. Answer the following questions to the best of your ability. Some questions may be inconclusive.

2. **What** caused this to happen?

_____

_____

3. **Who** was involved or impacted?

_____

4. **Who** was responsible?

_____

5. **How** does this event manifest in this life?

_____

_____

_____

6. On a scale of **1 to 10**, with **10** being _"I am fully able to see how this narrative impacts me now,"_ and **1** being, _"I'm unsure how this narrative impacts me now,"_ how connected did you feel to this spread?

1   2   3   4   5   6   7   8   9   10

Day 6: Narrative Spread 3

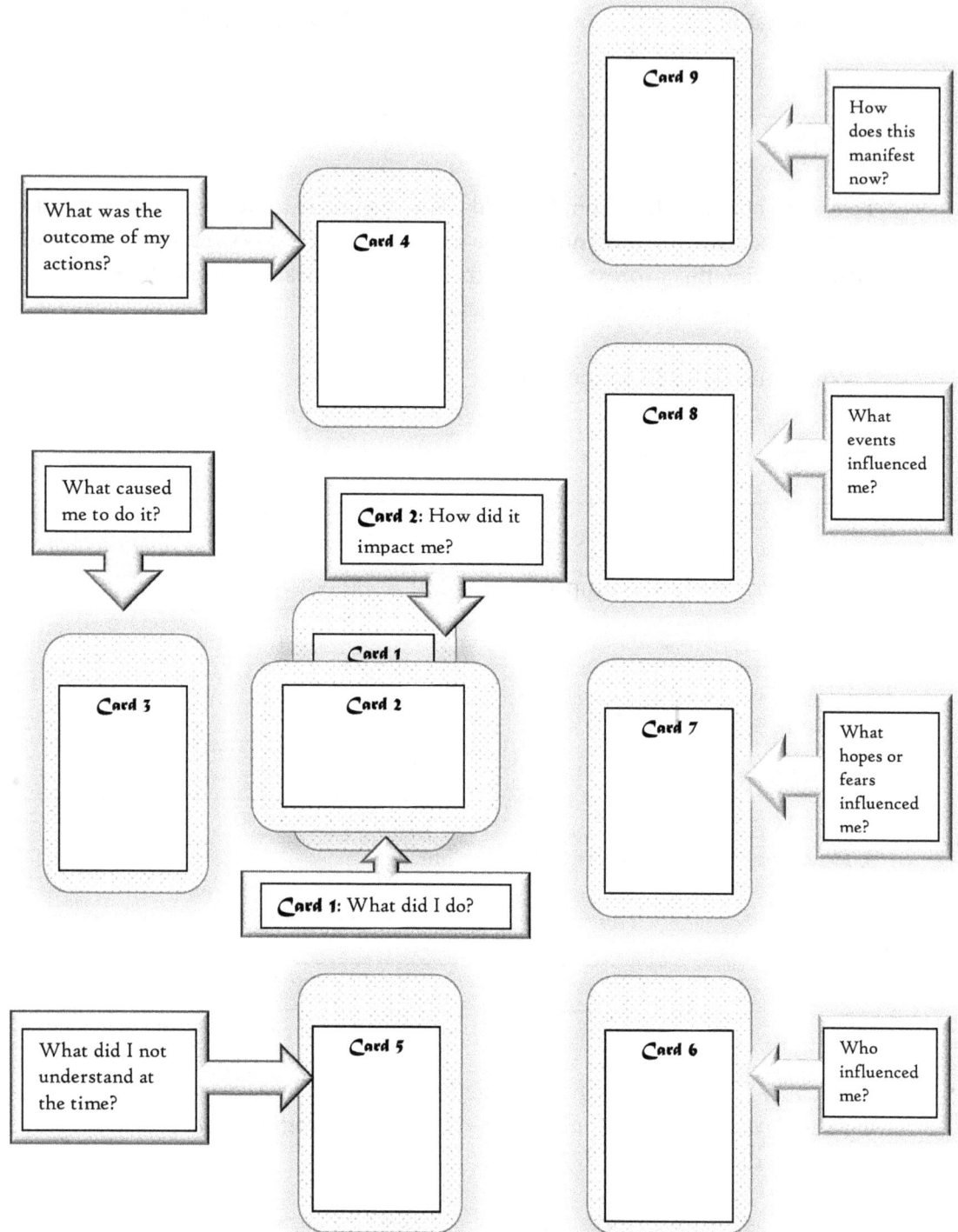

Card 9

How does this manifest now?

What was the outcome of my actions?

Card 4

Card 8

What events influenced me?

What caused me to do it?

Card 2: How did it impact me?

Card 1

Card 3

Card 2

Card 7

What hopes or fears influenced me?

Card 1: What did I do?

What did I not understand at the time?

Card 5

Card 6

Who influenced me?

Deconstruction/Application Day 6

1. **What did I do?**   **How it impacted me**

_____   _____

To construct a narrative from the cards, you may need to deviate from some of the placements if it makes more sense to do so. Lean heavily on images and your instinct during this process.

2. **What** caused me to do it?

_____

3. **What** was the <u>outcome</u> of my actions?

_____

4. **What** did I not understand at the time?

_____

5. **How** does this event manifest in this life?

_____

Who influenced me	
What hopes or fears influenced me?	
What events influenced me?	

6. On a scale of **1 to 10**, with **10** being *"I am fully able to see how this narrative impacts me now,"* and **1** being, *"I'm unsure how this narrative impacts me now,"* how connected did you feel to this spread?

       1   2   3   4   5   6   7   8   9   10

Day 7: Spiritual Blockage Spread 1

For this spread, you are working to identify what your spiritual blockages may be and looking for insight that will help you form breakthroughs. Spiritual blockages are deep psychological beliefs or fears that are preventing your spiritual progression.

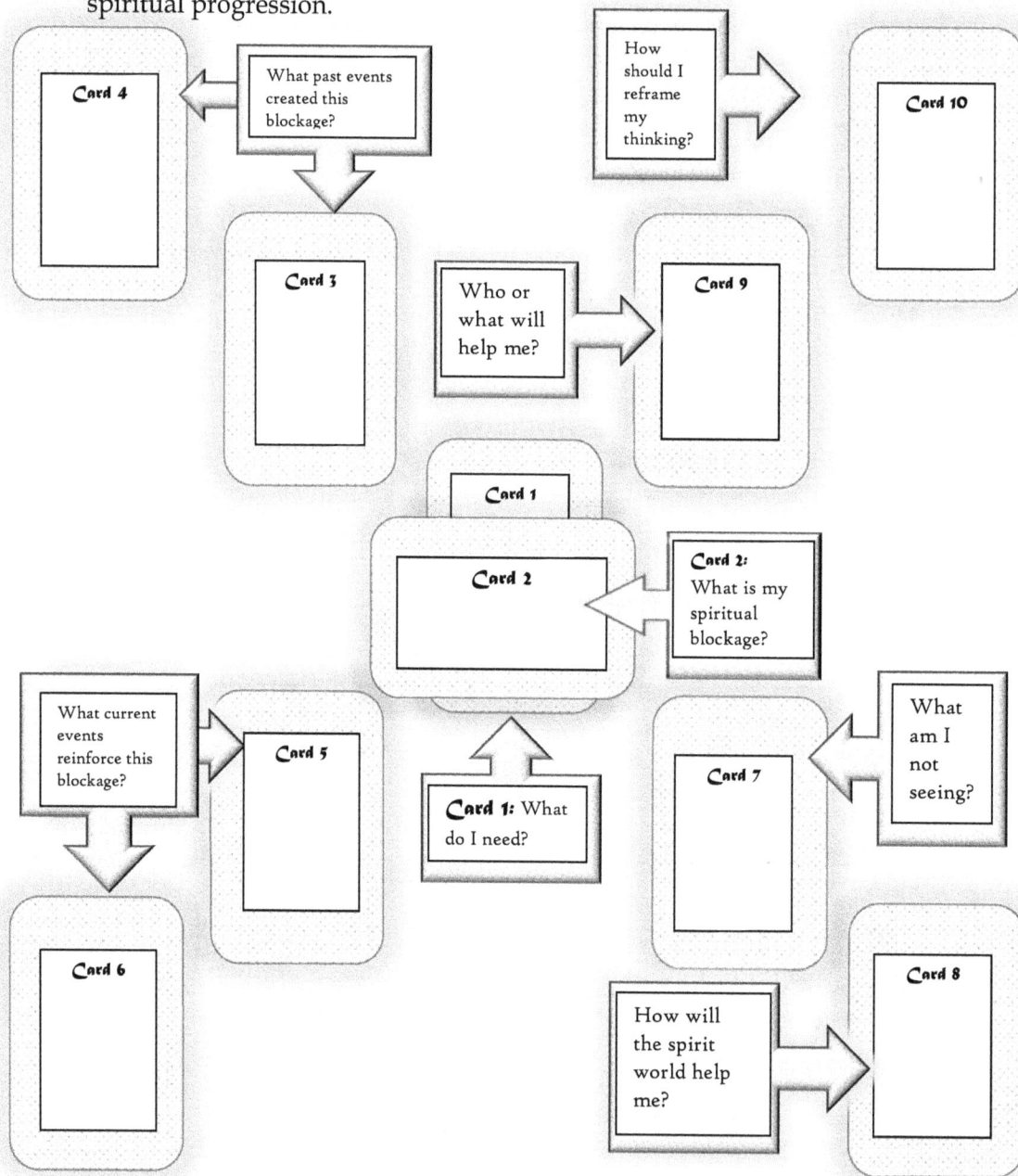

Card 4

What past events created this blockage?

How should I reframe my thinking?

Card 10

Card 3

Who or what will help me?

Card 9

Card 1

Card 2

Card 2: What is my spiritual blockage?

What current events reinforce this blockage?

Card 5

Card 7

What am I not seeing?

Card 1: What do I need?

Card 6

How will the spirit world help me?

Card 8

Deconstruction/Application Day 7

1.   **What do I need?**   **What is my spiritual blockage?**

_____   _____

2. **What** past life events created this blockage?

_____

_____

3. **What** current life events reinforced this blockage?

_____

_____

4. **What** am I not seeing?

_____

5. **How** will the spirit world help me?

_____

6. **Who** or **what** in the physical world will help me?

_____

7. **How** should I reframe my thinking?

_____

_____

_____

8. On a scale of **1 to 10**, with **10** being _"I now have more clarity about my spiritual blockage and how to address it,"_ and **1** being, _"I have no clarity about my spiritual blockages"_ how connected did you feel to this spread?

1   2   3   4   5   6   7   8   9   10

Day 8: Spiritual Blockage Spread 2

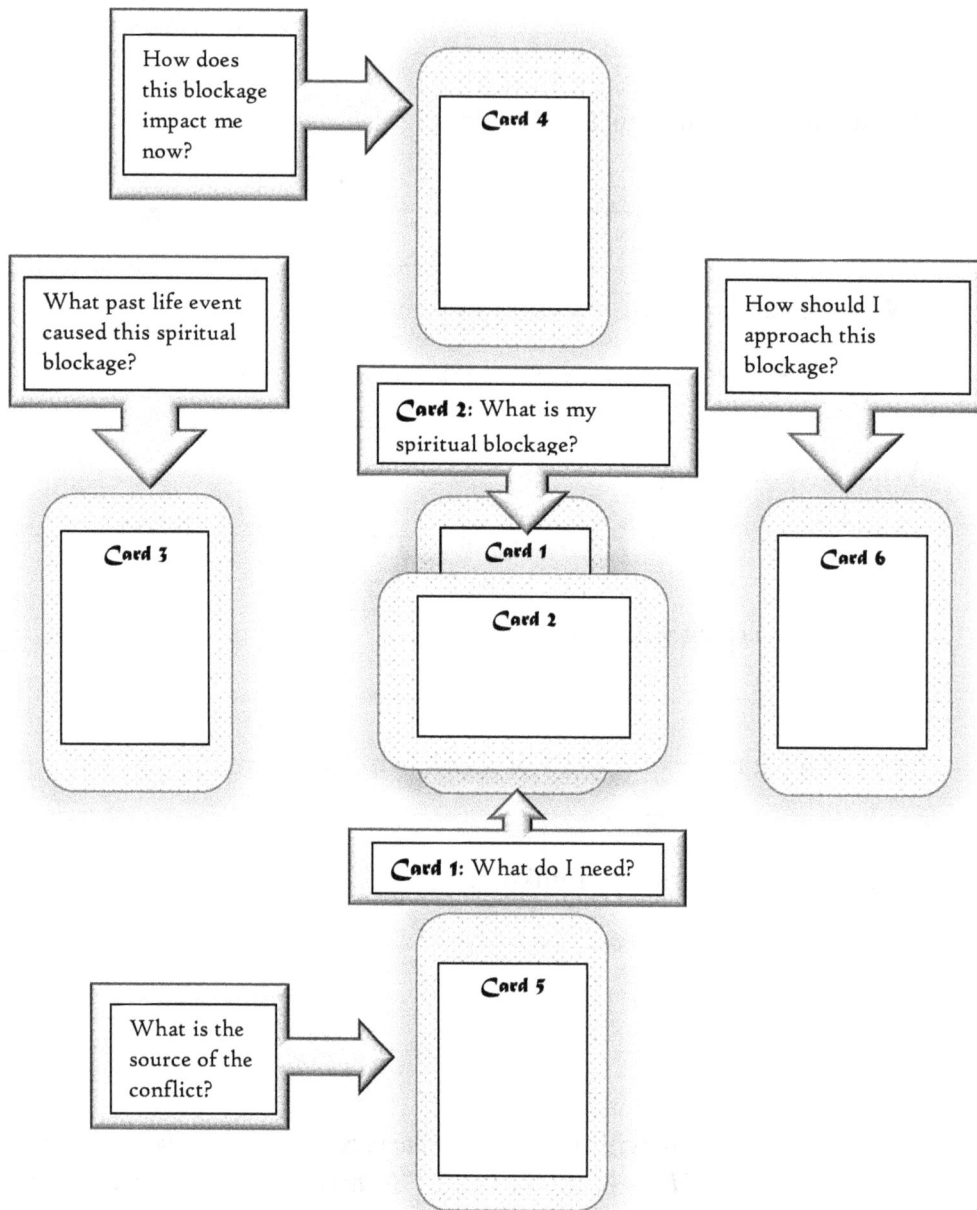

How does this blockage impact me now?

Card 4

What past life event caused this spiritual blockage?

Card 3

How should I approach this blockage?

Card 2: What is my spiritual blockage?

Card 1

Card 2

Card 6

Card 1: What do I need?

What is the source of the conflict?

Card 5

Deconstruction/Application Day 8

1.   **What do I need?**   **What is my spiritual blockage?**

_____   _____

2. **What** past life <u>event</u> created this blockage?

_____

_____

3. **How** does this blockage impact me now?

_____

_____

4. **What** is the <u>source</u> of the conflict?

_____

_____

5. **How** should I approach this blockage?

_____

6. Was there any repetition from the previous spread? Note either repeating cards or repeating energy/messages

_____

_____

7. Greatest insight from this spread:

_____

_____

_____

8. On a scale of **1 to 10**, with **10** being _"I now have more clarity about my spiritual blockage and how to address it,"_ and **1** being, _"I have no clarity about my spiritual blockages"_ how connected did you feel to this spread?

1   2   3   4   5   6   7   8   9   10

Day 9: Spiritual Blockage Spread 3

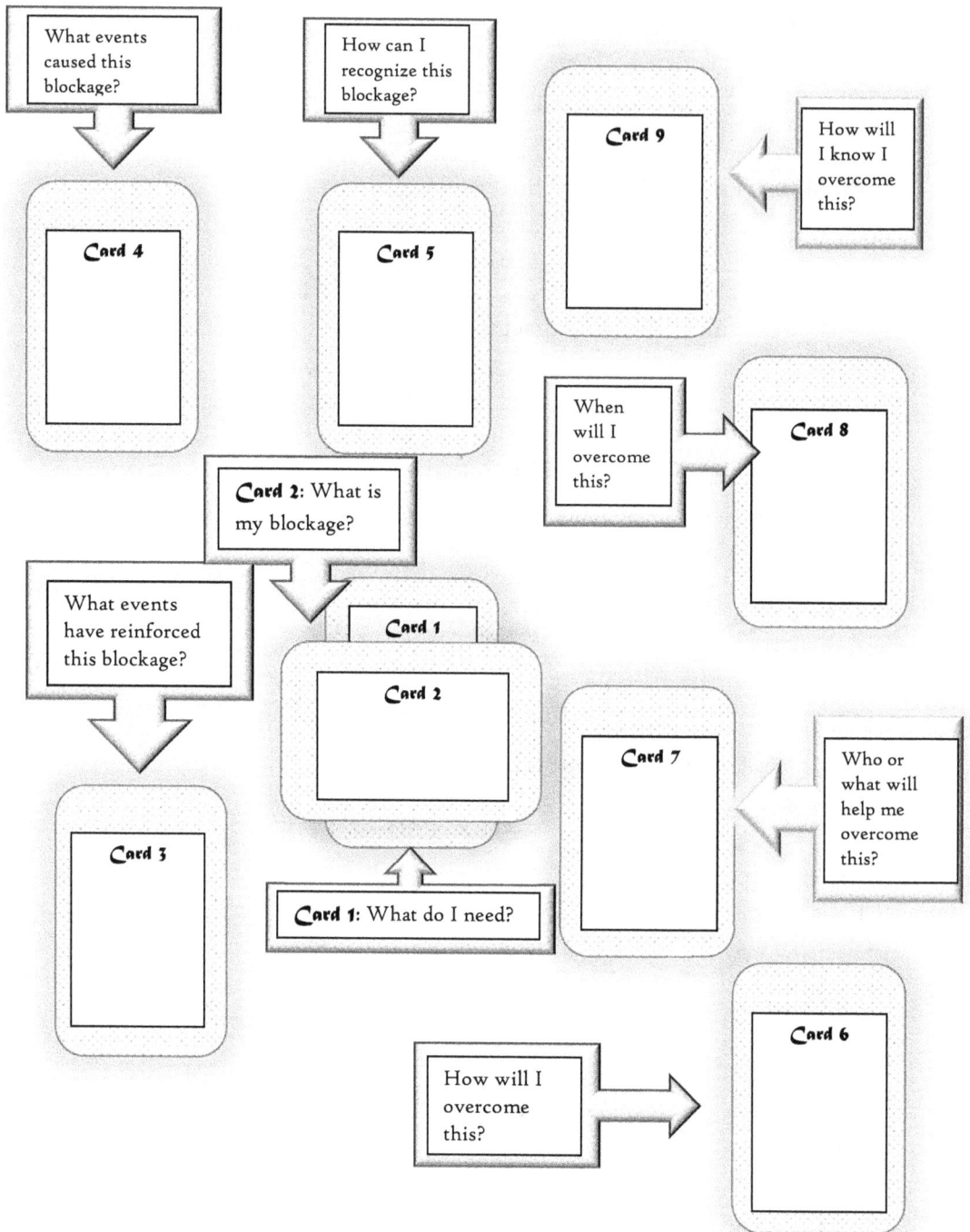

What events caused this blockage?

How can I recognize this blockage?

Card 9

How will I know I overcome this?

Card 4

Card 5

When will I overcome this?

Card 8

Card 2: What is my blockage?

What events have reinforced this blockage?

Card 1

Card 2

Card 7

Who or what will help me overcome this?

Card 3

Card 1: What do I need?

Card 6

How will I overcome this?

Deconstruction/Application Day 9

1.   **What do I need?**   **What is my spiritual blockage?**

_____   _____

2. **What** event <u>caused</u> this blockage?

_____

_____

3. **What** event <u>reinforced</u> this blockage?

_____

_____

4. **How** can I <u>recognize</u> this blockage?

_____

_____

5. **How** will I <u>overcome</u> this blockage?

_____

6. **Who** or **what** will help me?

_____

_____

7. **When** or **how** will I know I've overcome this blockage?

_____

_____

8. On a scale of **1 to 10**, with **10** being *"I now have more clarity about my spiritual blockage and how to address it,"* and **1** being, *"I have no clarity about my spiritual blockages"* how connected did you feel to this spread?

1   2   3   4   5   6   7   8   9   10

Day 10: Relationship Spread 1 General Karmic

Use this spread to look at the history of a relationship with someone that has not been very healthy or uplifting to you personally.

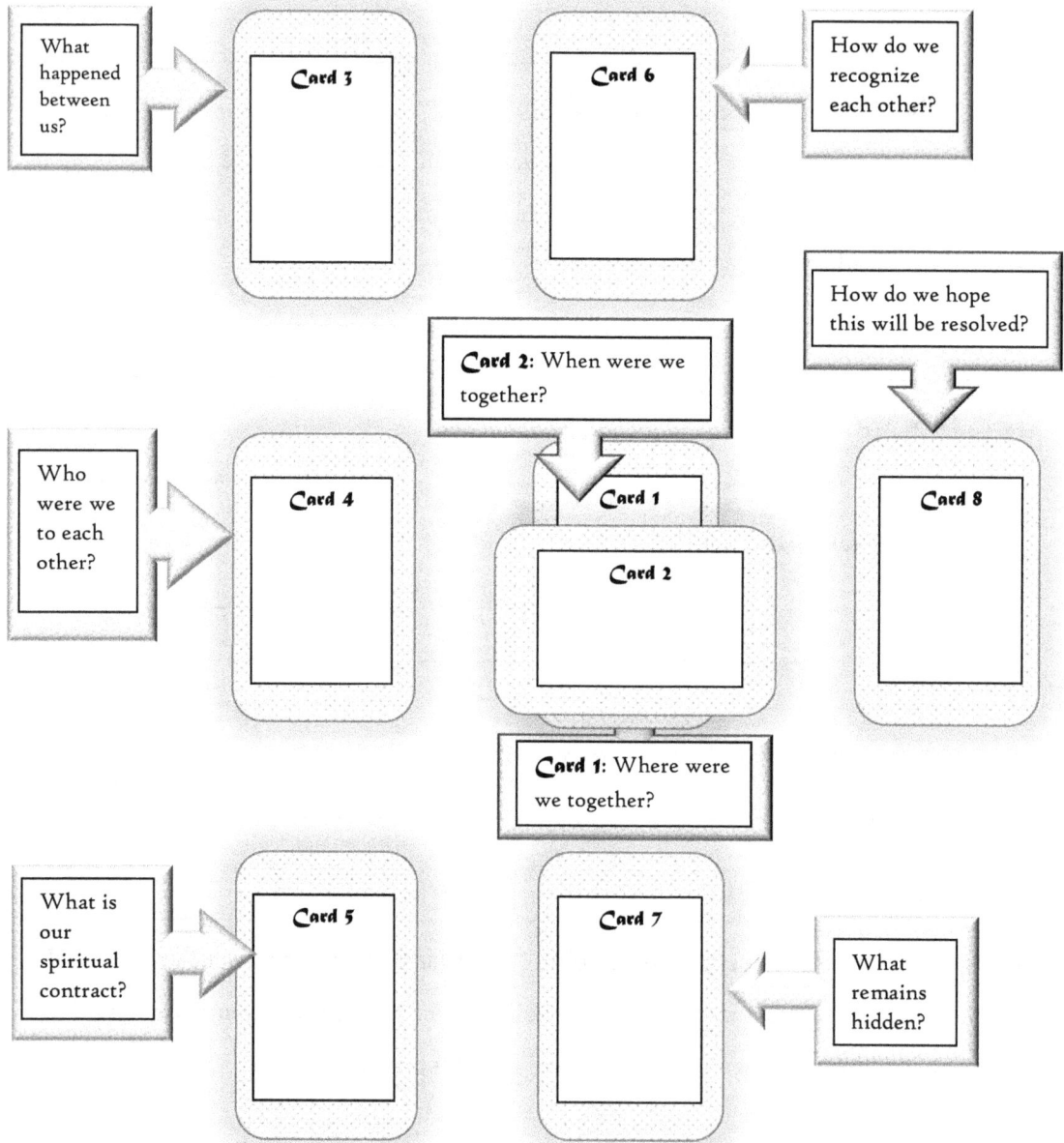

What happened between us? → **Card 3**

Card 6 ← How do we recognize each other?

How do we hope this will be resolved? →

Card 2: When were we together?

↓

Card 1

Who were we to each other? → **Card 4**

Card 2

Card 8

Card 1: Where were we together?

What is our spiritual contract? → **Card 5**

Card 7 ← What remains hidden?

Deconstruction/Application Day 10

1. **Where**   **When**

_____   _____

Note: You can use cards **1** and **2** interchangeably for place and time. Feel free to use surrounding cards for place and time as well if it makes more sense. If you are using a regular tarot deck, instead ask, _"What was going on in history during this time?"_

Name or initials of the person I'm reading on: _____

2. **What** happened between us?

_____

3. **Who** were we to each other?

_____

4. **What** is our <u>spiritual contract</u>?

_____

5. **How** do we recognize each other?

_____

8. **What** remains hidden?

_____

9. **How** do we hope this will be resolved?

_____

8. On a scale of **1 to 10**, with **10** being _"I've gained substantial spiritual insight into my relationship with this person,"_ and **1** being, _"I have gained no spiritual insight into this relationship,"_ how connected did you feel to this spread?

1   2   3   4   5   6   7   8   9   10

Day 11: Relationship Spread 2 Family/Friend

Use this spread for a healthy/happy relationship. This can be used for a romantic relationship as well, but better suited for a long-term romantic relationship.

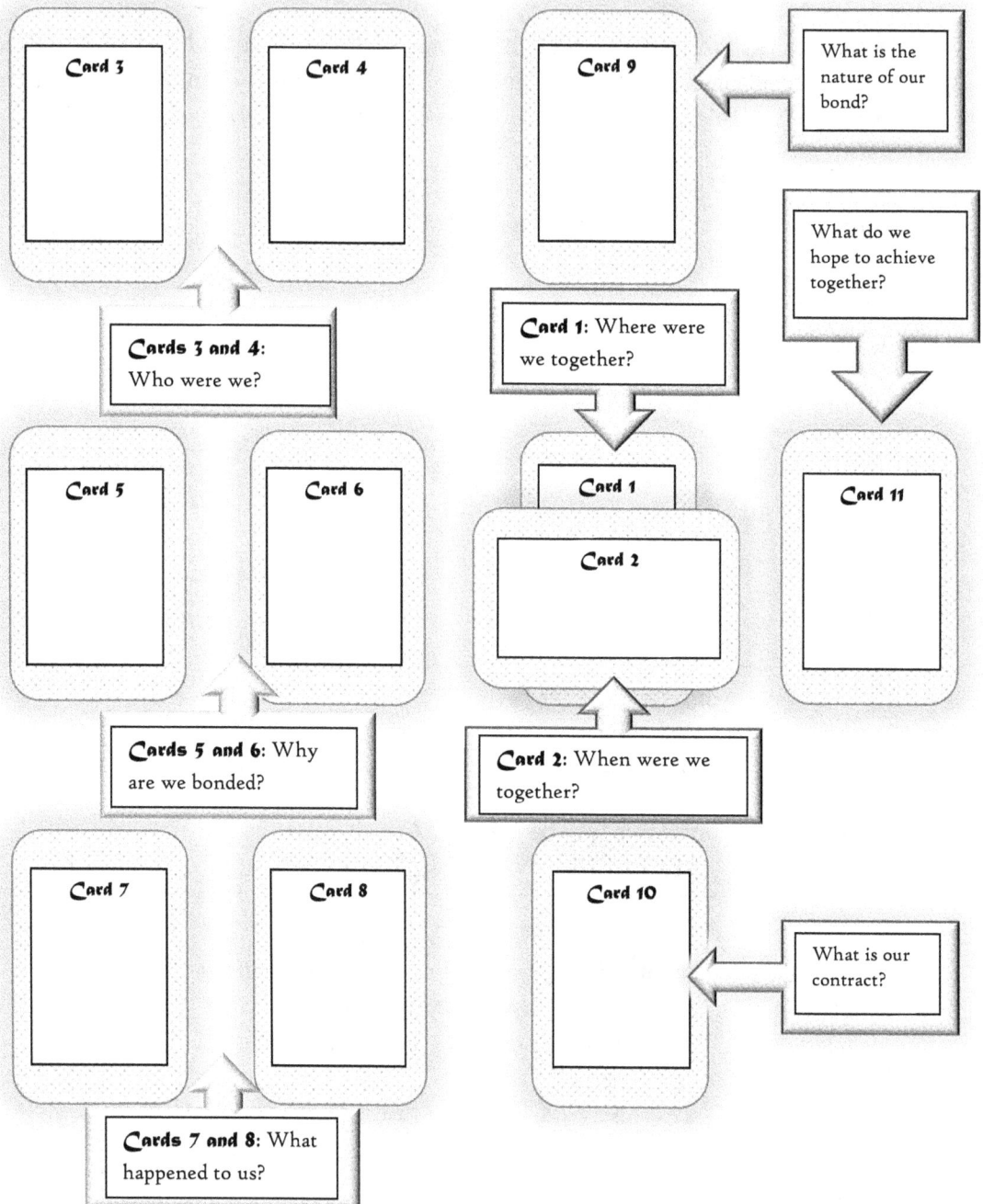

Card 3

Card 4

Card 9

What is the nature of our bond?

Cards 3 and 4: Who were we?

Card 1: Where were we together?

What do we hope to achieve together?

Card 5

Card 6

Card 1

Card 2

Card 11

Cards 5 and 6: Why are we bonded?

Card 2: When were we together?

Card 7

Card 8

Card 10

What is our contract?

Cards 7 and 8: What happened to us?

Deconstruction/Application Day 11

1.   **Where**   **When**

_____   _____

Note: You can use cards 1 and 2 interchangeably for place and time. Feel free to use surrounding cards for place and time as well if it makes more sense. If you are using a regular tarot deck, instead ask, *"What was going on in history during this time?"*

Name or initials of the person I'm reading on: _____

2. **Who** were we to each other?
_____

3. **Why** are we bonded?
_____

4. **What** happened to us?
_____

5. **What** is the nature of our bond?
_____

8. **What** is our contract?
_____

9. **What** do we hope to accomplish together?

_____

8. On a scale of **1 to 10**, with **10** being *"I've gained substantial spiritual insight into my relationship with this person,"* and **1** being, *"I have gained no spiritual insight into this relationship,"* how connected did you feel to this spread?

       1   2   3   4   5   6   7   8   9   10

Day 12: Relationship Spread 3 Romantic

Use this spread for a short-term romantic relationship, or a romantic relationship with serious issues/unhealthy dynamics.

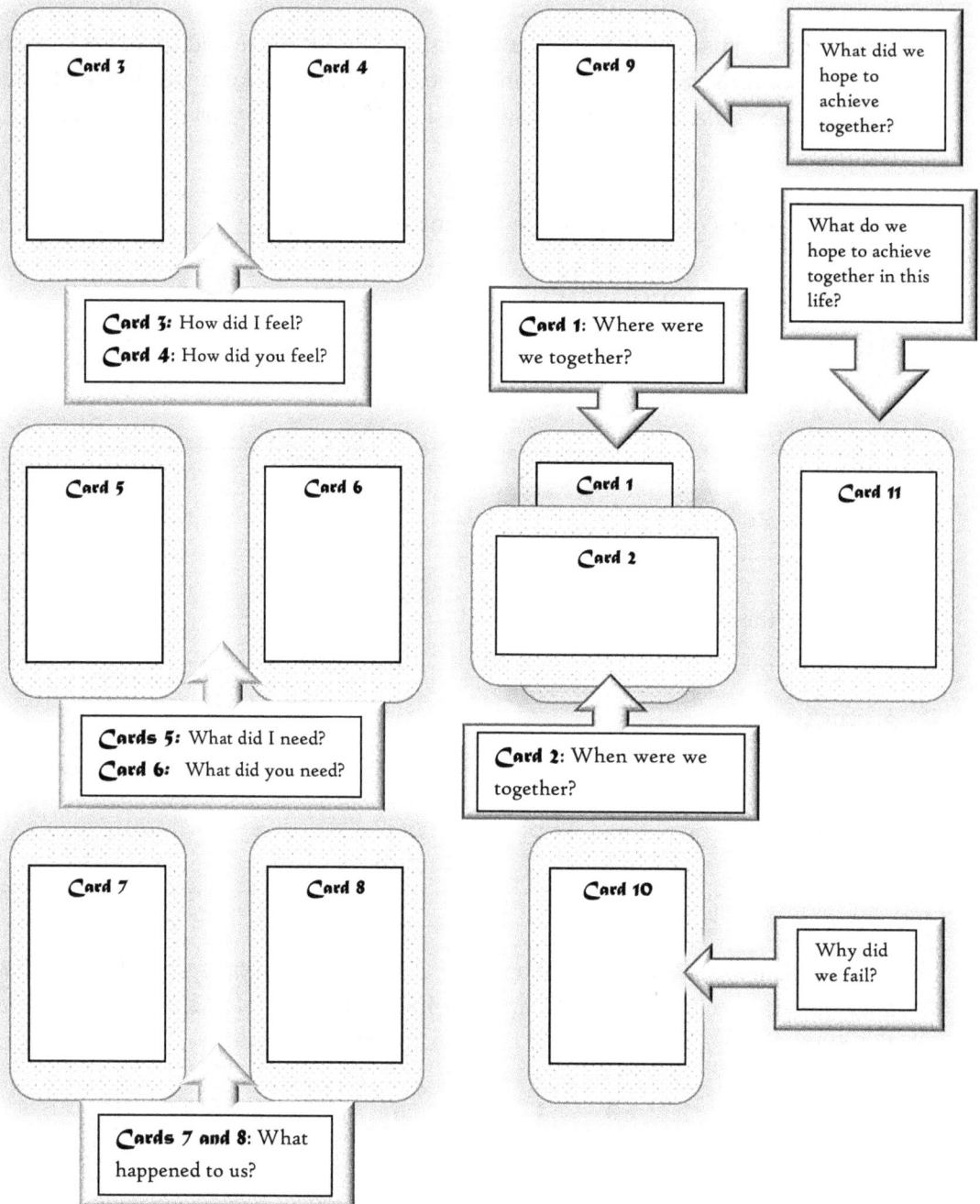

Card 3

Card 4

Card 9

What did we hope to achieve together?

Card 3: How did I feel?

Card 4: How did you feel?

Card 1: Where were we together?

What do we hope to achieve together in this life?

Card 5

Card 6

Card 1

Card 11

Card 2

Cards 5: What did I need?

Card 6: What did you need?

Card 2: When were we together?

Card 7

Card 8

Card 10

Why did we fail?

Cards 7 and 8: What happened to us?

Deconstruction/Application Day 12

1. **Where**   **When**

_____   _____

Note: You can use cards 1 and 2 interchangeably for place and time. Feel free to use surrounding cards for place and time as well if it makes more sense. If you are using a regular tarot deck, instead ask, _"What was going on in history during this time?"_

Name or initials of the person I'm reading on: _____

How I felt about you in this relationship	How you felt about me in this relationship
What I needed from the relationship	What you needed from the relationship

2. **What** did we hope to achieve together in this past life?

_____

3. **Why** did we fail?

_____

4. **What** do we hope to achieve together in this life?

_____

5. On a scale of **1 to 10**, with **10** being _"I've gained substantial spiritual insight into my relationship with this person,"_ and **1** being, _"I have gained no spiritual insight into this relationship,"_ how connected did you feel to this spread?

     1   **2**   **3**   **4**   **5**   **6**   **7**   **8**   **9**   **10**

Day 13: Phobias and Fears Spread 1

This spread is best for identifying a fear rather than looking more deeply at a fear you are aware of.

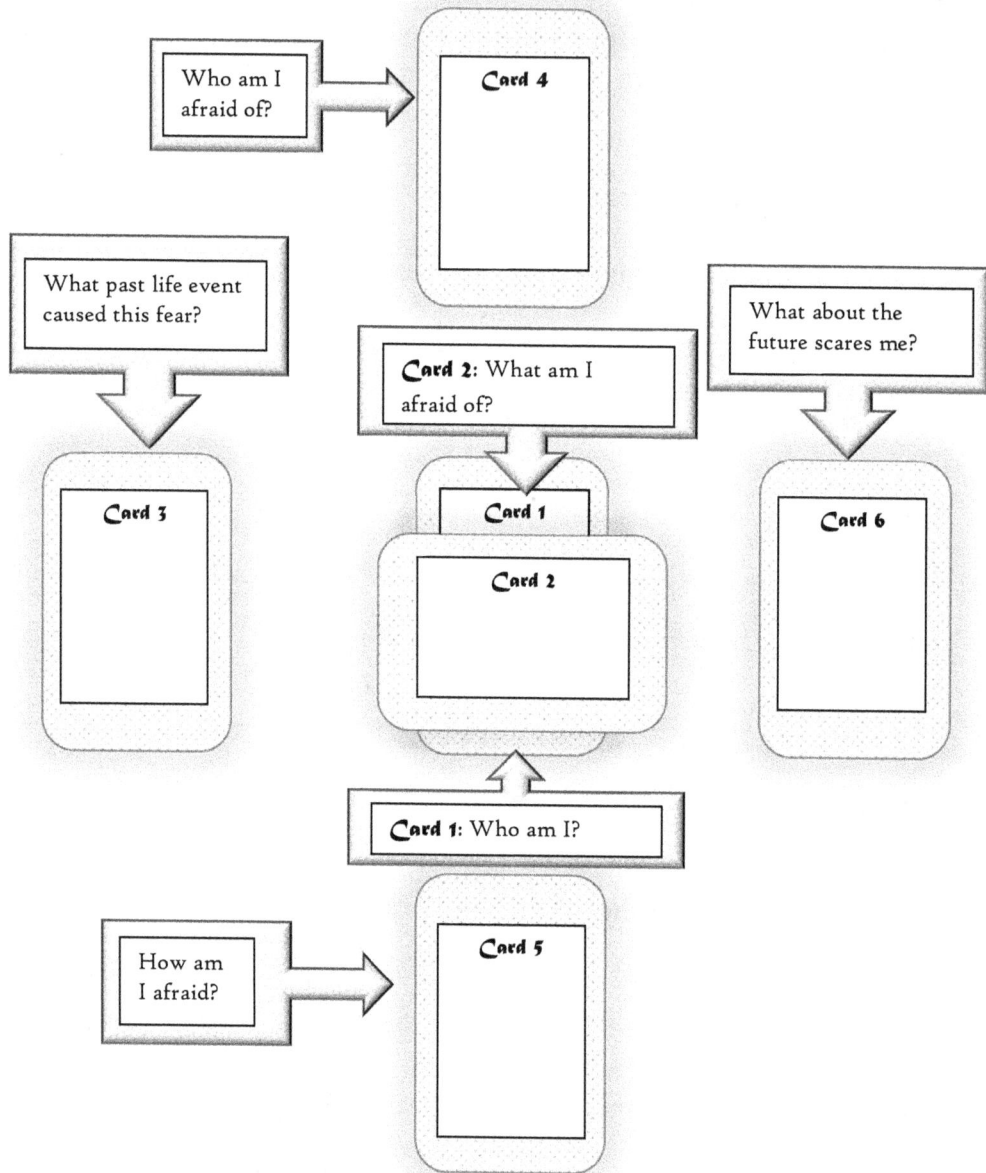

| Who am I afraid of? |
| → Card 4 |

| What past life event caused this fear? |
| Card 3 |

| Card 2: What am I afraid of? |
| Card 1 |
| Card 2 |

| What about the future scares me? |
| Card 6 |

| Card 1: Who am I? |

| How am I afraid? |
| Card 5 |

Deconstruction/Application Day 13

1.　　**Who am I?**　　　　　　　　　　**What am I afraid of?**

_____　　　_____

2. Read cards **1** and **2** as a combination. What about your spiritual essence is influenced or characterized by this fear?

_____

_____

_____

What past life event caused this fear?	Who am I afraid of?
How am I afraid? (triggers)	What about the future scares me?

3. On a scale of **1 to 10**, with **10** being _"I've uncovered and identified a recognizable fear,"_ and **1** being, _"I have no concrete leads on what my fears might be,"_ how connected did you feel to this spread?

　　　　1　　2　　3　　4　　5　　6　　7　　8　　9　　10

Day 14: Phobias and Fears Spread 2

Root-Focused

Use this spread to look closely at the cause of your fear or phobia.

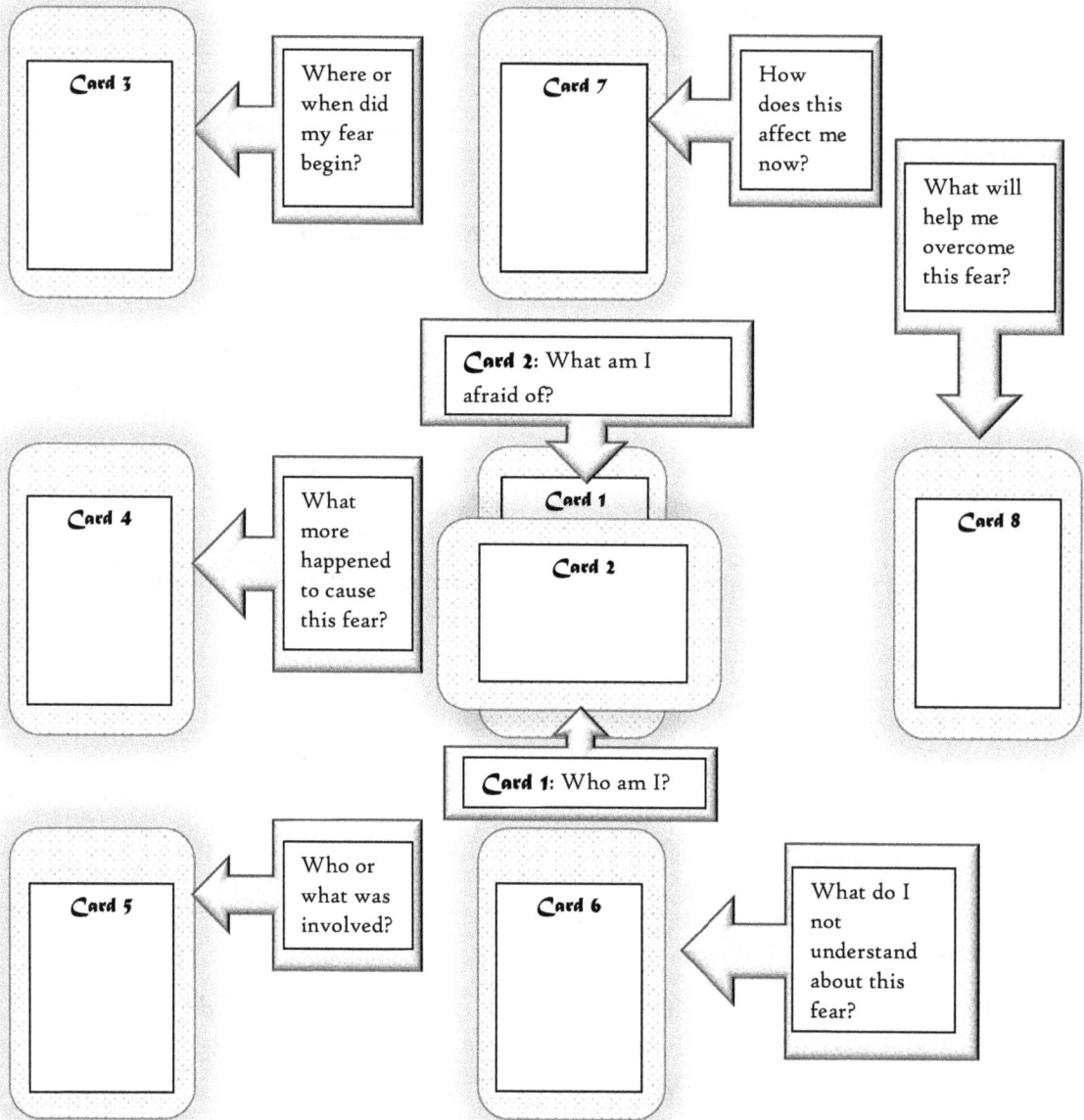

Card 3

Where or when did my fear begin?

Card 7

How does this affect me now?

What will help me overcome this fear?

Card 2: What am I afraid of?

Card 4

What more happened to cause this fear?

Card 1

Card 2

Card 8

Card 1: Who am I?

Card 5

Who or what was involved?

Card 6

What do I not understand about this fear?

Deconstruction/Application Day 14

1.   **Who am I?**   **What am I afraid of?**

_____   _____

2. Read cards **1** and **2** as a combination. What about your spiritual essence is influenced or characterized by this fear?

_____
_____
_____

Where or when did this fear begin?	What more happened to cause this fear?
Who or what was involved?	What do I not understand?
How does this affect me now?	How will I overcome this fear?

3. On a scale of **1 to 10**, with **10** being _"I've uncovered and identified a recognizable fear,"_ and **1** being, _"I have no concrete leads on what my fears might be,"_ how connected did you feel to this spread?

       1   2   3   4   5   6   7   8   9   10

Day 15: Phobias and Fears Spread 3

Healing-Focused

Use this spread to look closely at solutions for overcoming this phobia or fear.

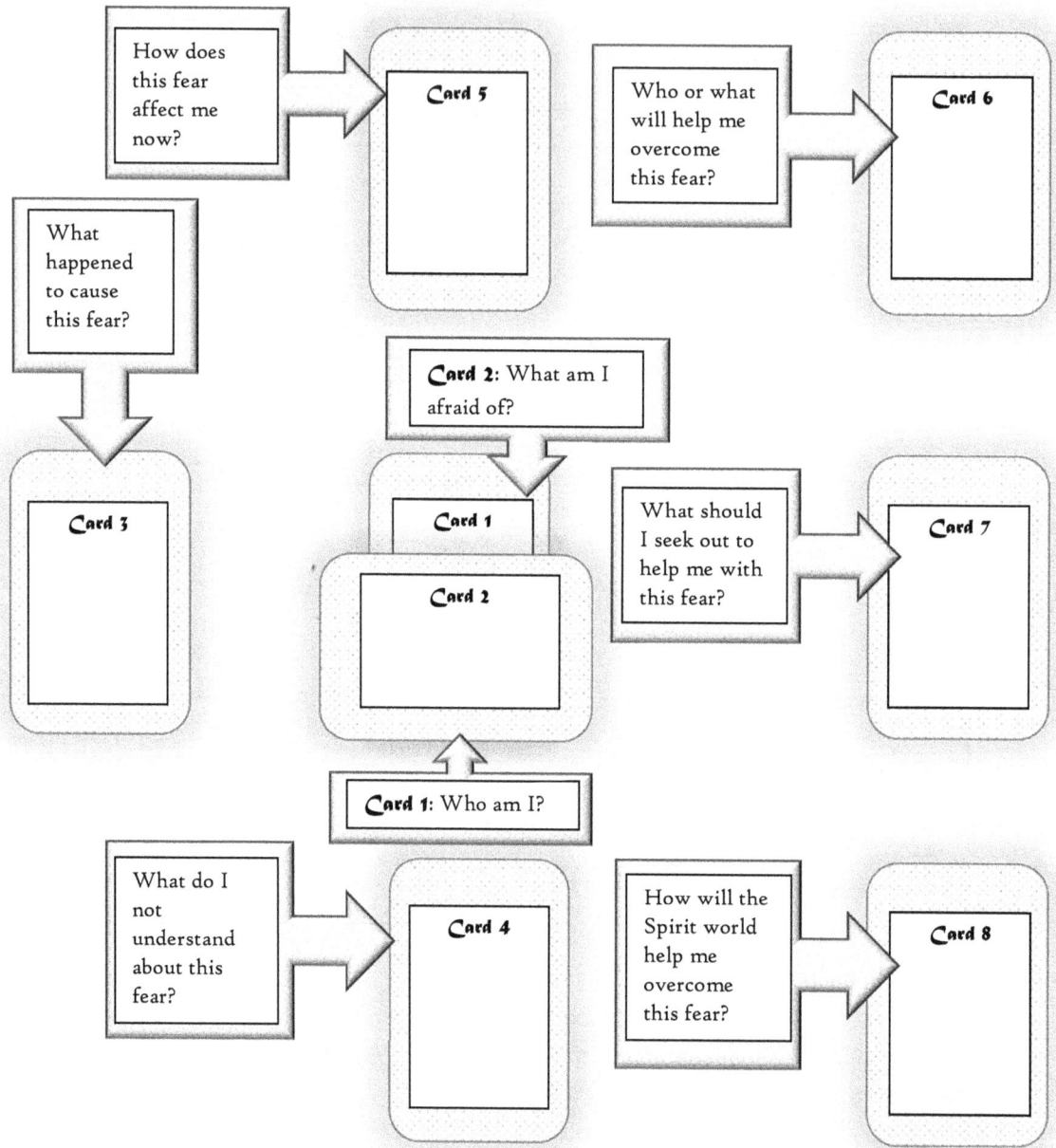

How does this fear affect me now? → Card 5

Who or what will help me overcome this fear? → Card 6

What happened to cause this fear? → Card 3

Card 2: What am I afraid of?

Card 1

Card 2

What should I seek out to help me with this fear? → Card 7

Card 1: Who am I?

What do I not understand about this fear? → Card 4

How will the Spirit world help me overcome this fear? → Card 8

Deconstruction/Application Day 15

1. **Who am I?**   **What am I afraid of?**

    _____   _____

2. Read cards **1** and **2** as a combination. What about your spiritual essence is influenced or characterized by this fear?

    _____

    _____

    _____

What happened to cause this fear?	How does this affect me now?
What do I not understand?	Who or what will help me overcome this fear?
What should I seek out to help me with this fear?	How will the spirit world help me overcome this fear?

1. On a scale of **1 to 10**, with **10** being _"I've uncovered and identified a recognizable fear,"_ and **1** being, _"I have no concrete leads on what my fears might be,"_ how connected did you feel to this spread?

    1   2   3   4   5   6   7   8   9   10

Day 16: Dreams Spread 1 Consciousness Spread

Use a selected dream from your dream journal. Reflect on these three levels of consciousness in order to interpret the dream's deeper messages.

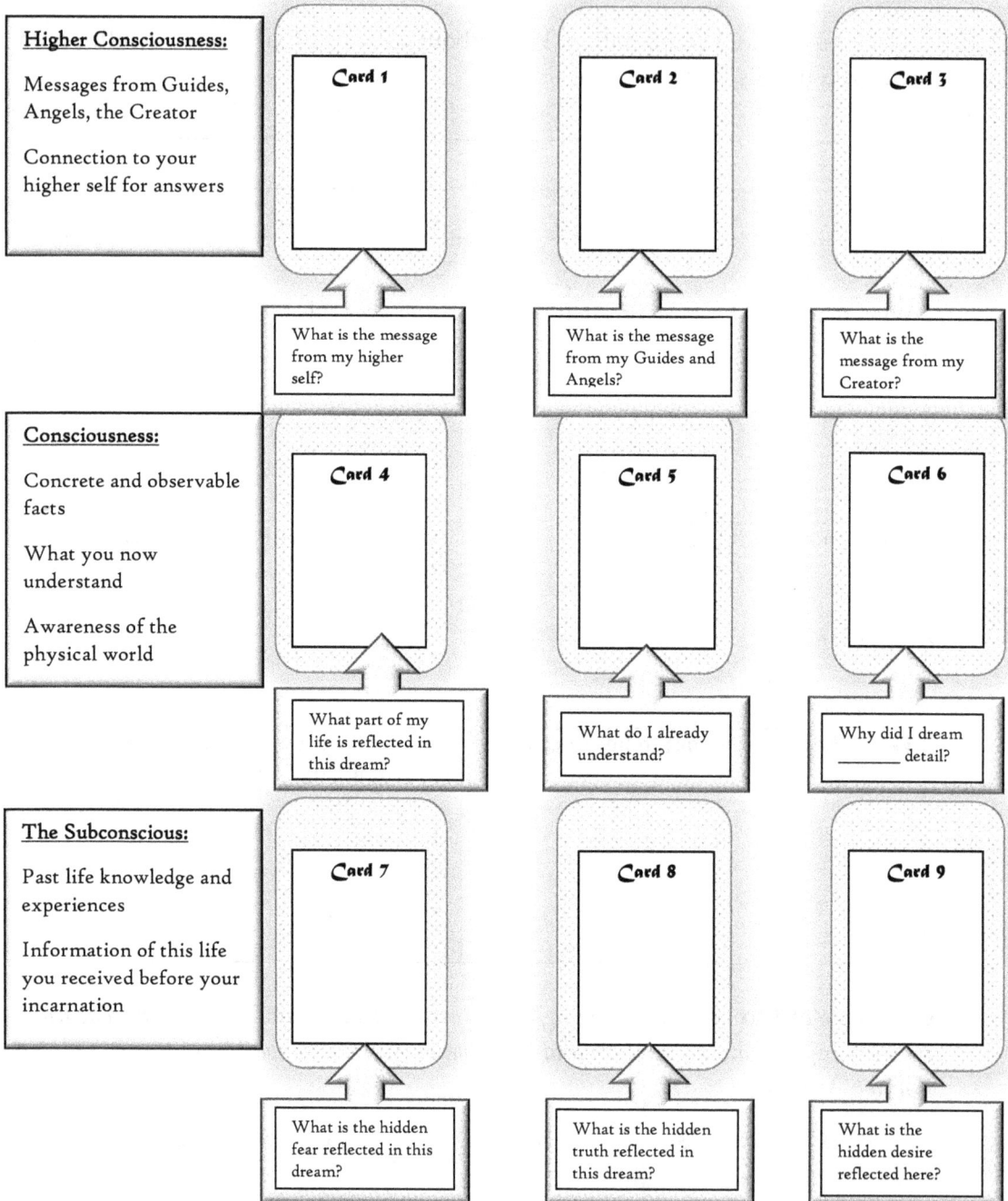

Higher Consciousness:

Messages from Guides, Angels, the Creator

Connection to your higher self for answers

Card 1

Card 2

Card 3

What is the message from my higher self?

What is the message from my Guides and Angels?

What is the message from my Creator?

Consciousness:

Concrete and observable facts

What you now understand

Awareness of the physical world

Card 4

Card 5

Card 6

What part of my life is reflected in this dream?

What do I already understand?

Why did I dream _____ detail?

The Subconscious:

Past life knowledge and experiences

Information of this life you received before your incarnation

Card 7

Card 8

Card 9

What is the hidden fear reflected in this dream?

What is the hidden truth reflected in this dream?

What is the hidden desire reflected here?

Deconstruction/Application Day 16

Higher Consciousness	What is the message from my higher self?	What is the message from my guides and angels?	What is the message from my creator?
Consciousness	What part of my life is reflected in this dream?	What do I already understand?	Why did I dream _____? (insert your specific detail (s)
The Subconscious	What is the hidden fear reflected in this dream?	What is the hidden truth reflected in this dream?	What is the hidden desire reflected here?

On a scale of **1 to 10**, with **10** being *"I fully understand the spiritual message behind this dream,"* and **1** being, *"I can make no spiritual connection to this dream,"* how connected did you feel to this spread?

1   2   3   4   5   6   7   8   9   10

Day 17: Dreams Spread 2 Advice Spread

Use this spread to interpret a dream as advice.

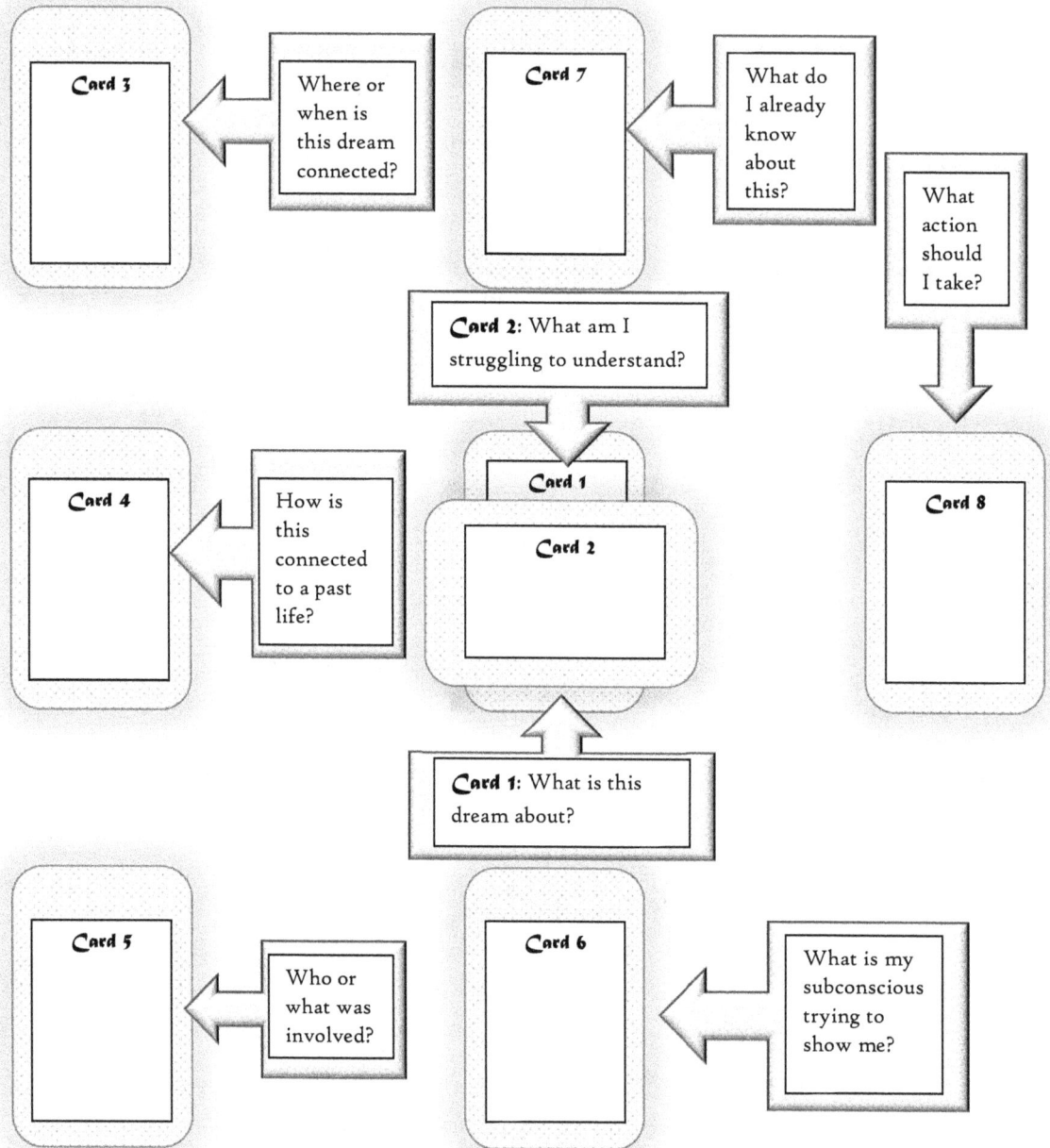

Card 3

Where or when is this dream connected?

Card 7

What do I already know about this?

What action should I take?

Card 2: What am I struggling to understand?

Card 4

How is this connected to a past life?

Card 1

Card 2

Card 8

Card 1: What is this dream about?

Card 5

Who or what was involved?

Card 6

What is my subconscious trying to show me?

Deconstruction/Application Day 17

1. What is the dream about?   What am I struggling to understand?

   _____   _____

2. Read cards **1** and **2** as a combination. What message do they offer when read together?

   _____

   _____

   _____

Where or when is this dream connected?	How is this connected to a past life?
Who or what was involved?	What do I already know about this issue?
What is my subconscious trying to show me?	What action should I take?

3. On a scale of **1 to 10**, with **10** being *"I fully understand the spiritual message behind this dream,"* and **1** being, *"I can make no spiritual connection to this dream,"* how connected did you feel to this spread?

     1   2   3   4   5   6   7   8   9   10

Day 18: Dreams Spread 3

Decoding the Message

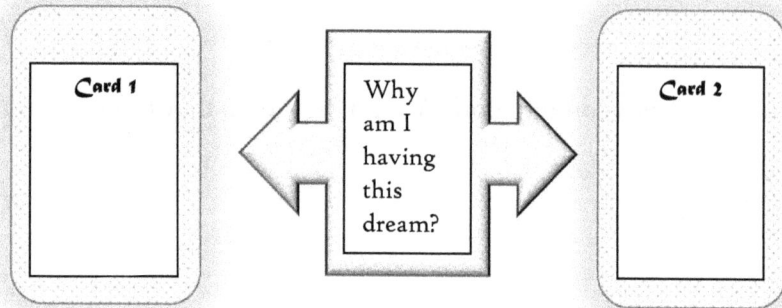

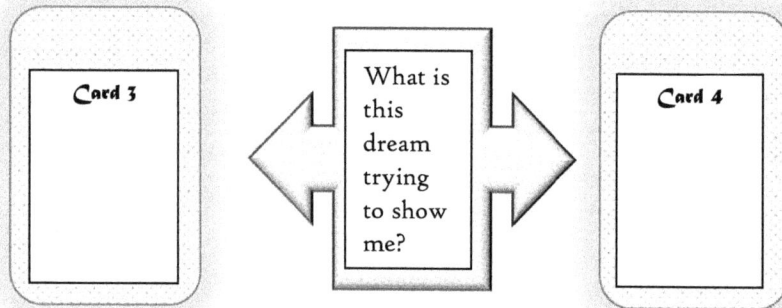

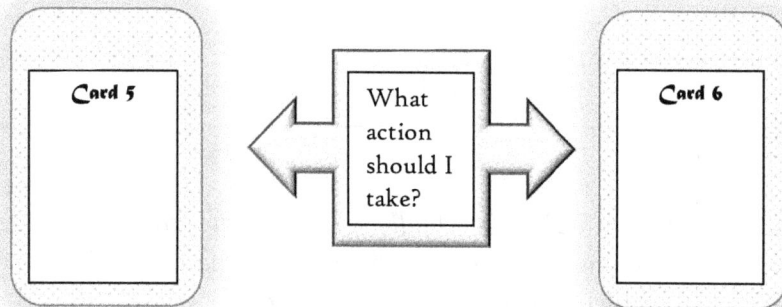

| Card 1 | Why am I having this dream? | Card 2 |

| Card 3 | What is this dream trying to show me? | Card 4 |

| Card 5 | What action should I take? | Card 6 |

Deconstruction/Application Day 18

Why am I having this dream? **Card 1**	Why am I having this dream? **Card 2**
Draw an interpretation to this question by reading these two cards in combination:	

What is this dream trying to show me? **Card 3**	What is this dream trying to show me? **Card 4**
Draw an interpretation to this question by reading these two cards in combination:	

What action should I take? **Card 5**	What action should I take? **Card 6**
Draw an interpretation to this question by reading these two cards in combination:	

On a scale of **1 to 10**, with **10** being "*I fully understand the spiritual message behind this dream,*" and **1** being, "*I can make no spiritual connection to this dream,*" how connected did you feel to this spread?

1   2   3   4   5   6   7   8   9   10

Day 19: Life Goals Spread 1

Identifying Your Goal(s)

You probably have more than one life goal. These spreads focus on one goal at time, so it might be helpful to do the spreads more than once. Select cards that represent your goal for spreads 2 and 3 once you have clarity about what your goals are.

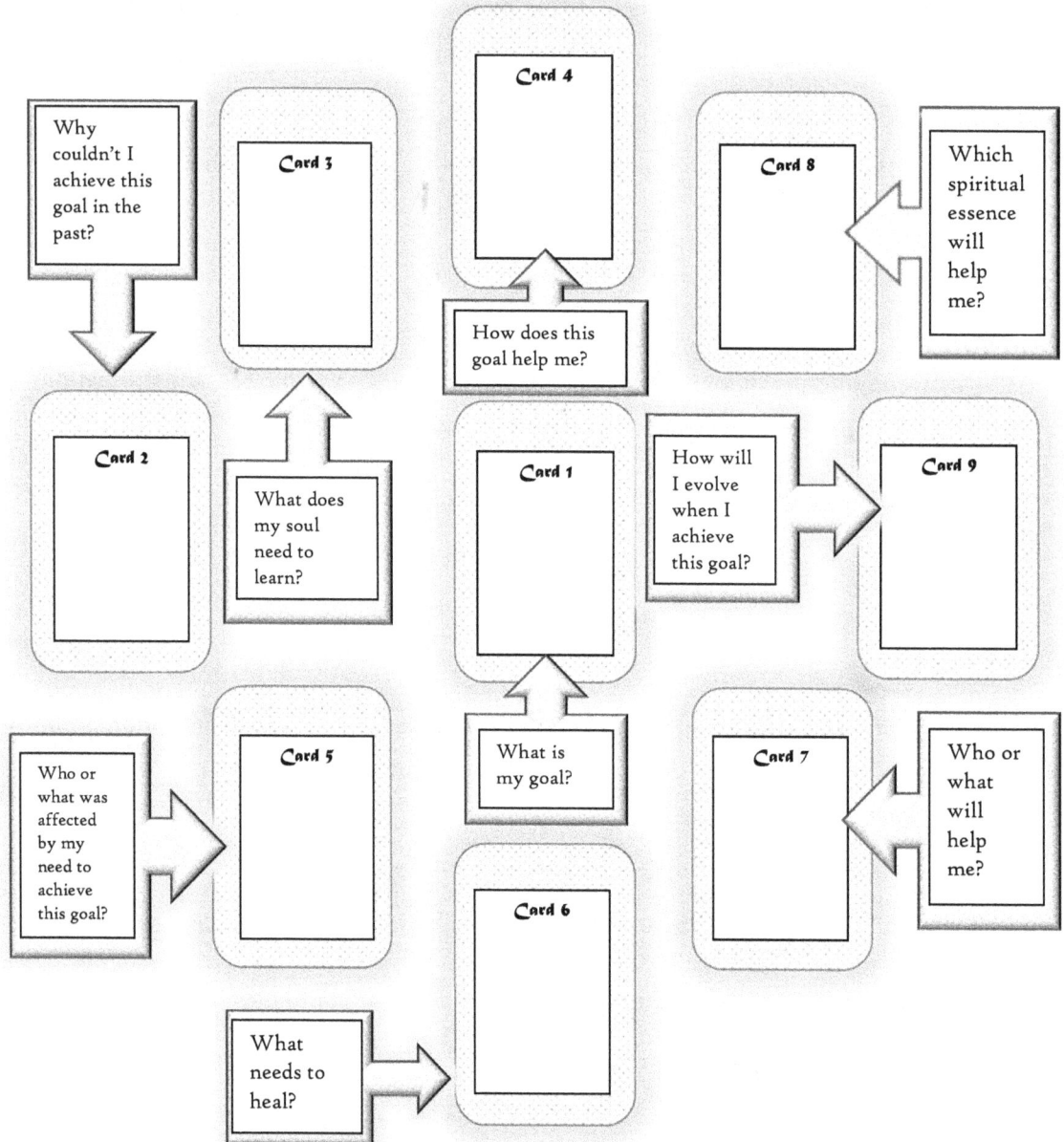

Card 4

Card 3

Why couldn't I achieve this goal in the past?

Card 8

Which spiritual essence will help me?

Card 2

How does this goal help me?

What does my soul need to learn?

Card 1

How will I evolve when I achieve this goal?

Card 9

Who or what was affected by my need to achieve this goal?

Card 5

What is my goal?

Card 7

Who or what will help me?

Card 6

What needs to heal?

Deconstruction/Application Day 19

1. What is my goal?

_____

The Past	The Present/Future
Why couldn't I achieve this goal in the past?	How does this goal help me?
What does my soul need to learn?	Which spiritual essence will help me?
Who or what was affected by my need to achieve this goal?	Who or what will help me?
What still needs to heal?	How will I evolve when I achieve this goal?

2. On a scale of **1 to 10**, with **10** being "_I have a clear vision of my lifetime's goals and how I will achieve them,_" and **1** being, "_I have no clarification about my lifetime's goals,_" how connected did you feel to this spread?

1   2   3   4   5   6   7   8   9   10

Day 20: Life Goals Spread 2

Understanding Why

For this spread, you will look at the energetic impacts of your goal, both past and future.

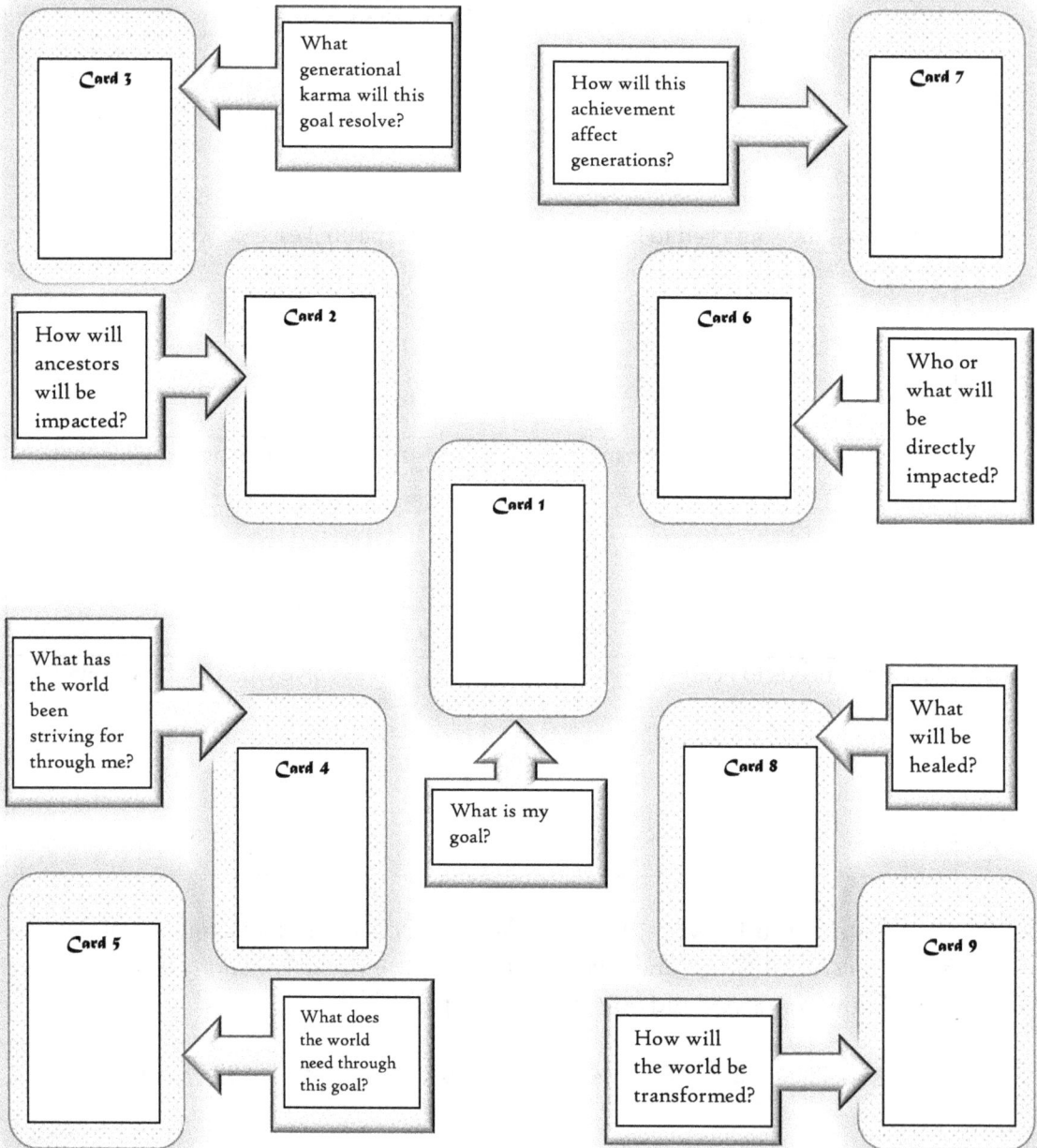

Card 3

What generational karma will this goal resolve?

How will this achievement affect generations?

Card 7

How will ancestors will be impacted?

Card 2

Card 6

Who or what will be directly impacted?

Card 1

What has the world been striving for through me?

Card 4

What is my goal?

Card 8

What will be healed?

Card 5

What does the world need through this goal?

Card 9

How will the world be transformed?

Deconstruction/Application Day 20

1.   **What is my goal?**

_____

How my goal will affect past karma	How my goal will affect the future
What generational karma will be resolved?	How will this achievement affect future generations?
How will my ancestors will be impacted?	Who or what will be impacted in the future?
What has the world been striving for through me?	What will be healed
What has the world needed through me?	How will the world be transformed?

2. On a scale of **1 to 10**, with **10** being _"I have a clear vision of my lifetime's goals and how I will achieve them,"_ and **1** being, _"I have no clarification about my lifetime's goals,"_ how connected did you feel to this spread?

   1   2   3   4   5   6   7   8   9   10

Day 21: Life Goals Spread 3

Progression of the Soul

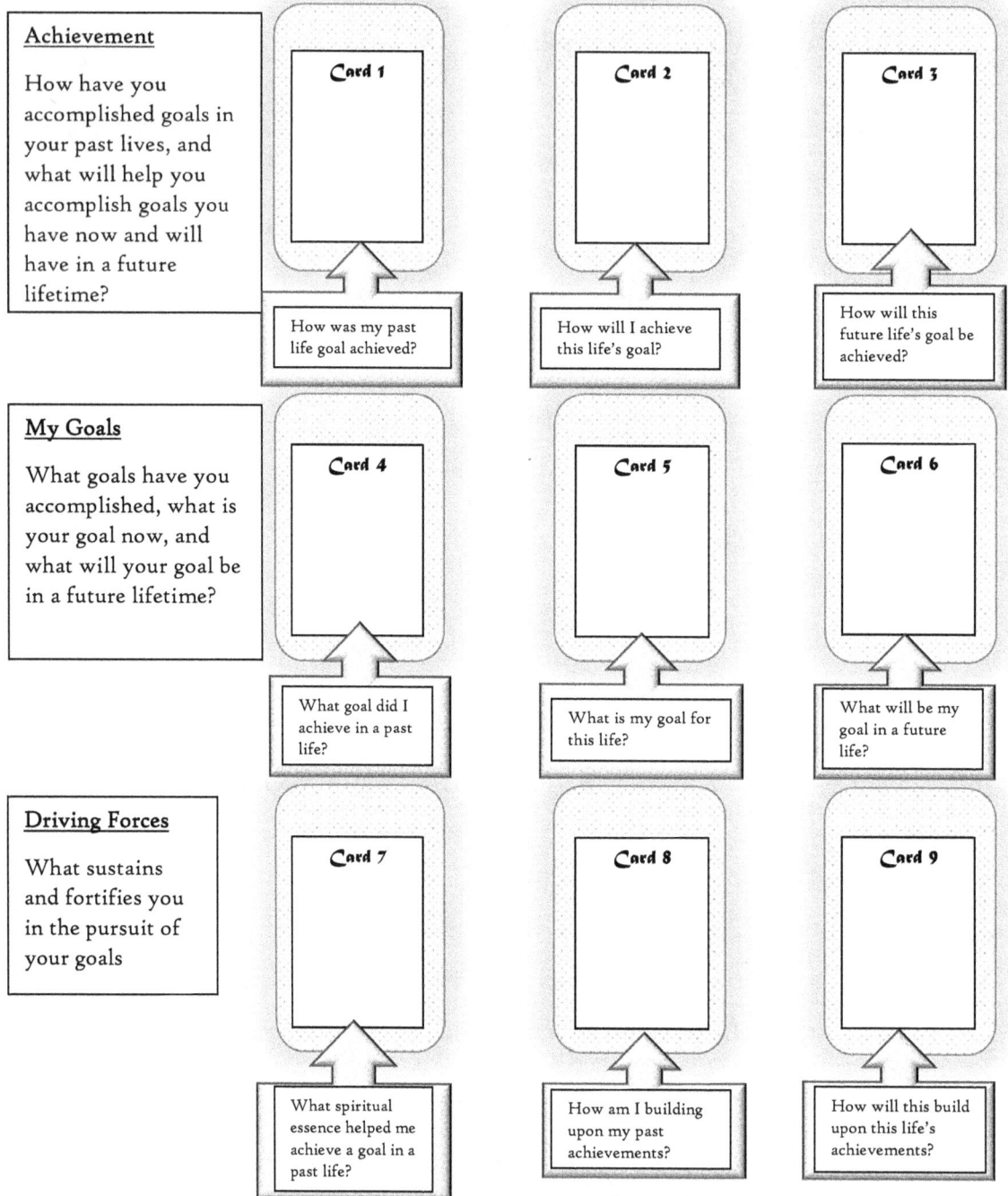

Achievement

How have you accomplished goals in your past lives, and what will help you accomplish goals you have now and will have in a future lifetime?

| Card 1 | Card 2 | Card 3 |

How was my past life goal achieved?

How will I achieve this life's goal?

How will this future life's goal be achieved?

My Goals

What goals have you accomplished, what is your goal now, and what will your goal be in a future lifetime?

| Card 4 | Card 5 | Card 6 |

What goal did I achieve in a past life?

What is my goal for this life?

What will be my goal in a future life?

Driving Forces

What sustains and fortifies you in the pursuit of your goals

| Card 7 | Card 8 | Card 9 |

What spiritual essence helped me achieve a goal in a past life?

How am I building upon my past achievements?

How will this build upon this life's achievements?

Deconstruction/Application Day 21

Achievements	How was my past life goal achieved?	How will I achieve this life's goal?	How will this future life's goal be achieved?
My Goals	What goal did I achieve in a past life?	What is my goal for this life?	What will be my goal in a future life?
Driving Forces	What spiritual essence helped me achieve a goal in a past life?	How am I building upon my past achievements?	How will this build upon this life's achievements?

On a scale of **1 to 10**, with **10** being *"I have a clear vision of my lifetime's goals and how I will achieve them,"* and **1** being, *"I have no clarification about my lifetime's goals,"* how connected did you feel to this spread?

1   2   3   4   5   6   7   8   9   10

Extra Visual/Language Worksheets

There are many ways to read cards, so you're going to practice these three main ways in order to learn what type of card reader you are. Also, the type of reader you are can shift and change as you practice, so I don't want you to think of this as a fixed truth.

1. Visual/Spiritual

For each of the cards, connect the images to your emotions. What do you feel when you look at this card? Forget, momentarily, what you know about the meaning of the cards or the words printed on them. Stay grounded in emotion/feelings, and what the image encourages you to feel, and not in ideas or language. Emotions are the language of Spirit, so you are most likely to make a connection and receive a message here, in this space.

A.) What did you feel while looking at the image on Card 1?

_____

_____

_____

B.) What did you feel while looking at the image on Card 2?

_____

_____

_____

After each reading, I want you to do a self-assessment to gauge your comfort level and success with this process.

C.) On a scale of **1 to 10**, with **10** being "*I was overcome with emotion and nearly brought to tears*" and **1** being "*I must be Vulcan*," how emotional did you feel looking at the image on <u>**Card 1**</u>?

1   2   3   4   5   6   7   8   9   10

D.) On a scale of **1 to 10**, with **10** being *"I was overcome with emotion and nearly brought to tears"* and **1** being *"I must be Vulcan,"* how emotional did you feel looking at the image on **Card 2**?

1   2   3   4   5   6   7   8   9   10

E.) On a scale of **1 to 10**, with **10** being *"I felt God/Goddess/Universe speaking directly to me through the card"* and **1** being *"This is only cardboard,"* how much of a spiritual connection did you feel gazing at the image on **Card 1**?

1   2   3   4   5   6   7   8   9   10

F.) On a scale of **1 to 10**, with **10** being *"I felt God/Goddess/Universe speaking directly to me through the card"* and **1** being *"This is only cardboard,"* how much of a spiritual connection did you feel gazing at the image on **Card 2**?

1   2   3   4   5   6   7   8   9   10

2. Language

Now you're going to focus on language in your response to the cards. You can examine what the language printed on the cards means outside of a tarot/oracle context, or you can focus on the language that is commonly associated with that card (this exercise will look vastly different depending on if you have experience with tarot or not).

A.) What are all the word/language associations you have with **Card 1**?

_____

_____

B.) What are all the word/language associations you have with **Card 2**?

_____

_____

I'd like you to build upon your existing knowledge of this language. Now, we are going to narrow the scope and shift away from every word association we might have, and instead focus on tarot/oracle interpretations. Get out the book that came with your deck, and pull out at least two more resources. These can be other books you have on hand, or websites. Research each of your cards and compare/contrast information between sources.

C.) What new language can you identify for **Card 1**?

_____

_____

D.) What new language can you identify for **Card 2**?

_____

_____

Next, let's make a comparison of all your language associations to your emotional response.

E.) When you compare your language associations to your emotional response for **Card 1**, how well do they align, if at all?

_____

_____

F.) When you compare your language associations to your emotional response for **Card 2**, how well do they align, if at all?

_____

_____

G.) On a scale of **1 to 10** with **10** being, "*My emotional response and language associations were completely in alignment*" to "*Neither card seemed to connect my emotional response to its intended meaning*," how well do you feel your spiritual and intellectual response to these two cards aligned?

1   2   3   4   5   6   7   8   9   10

Extra Visual/Language Worksheets

There are many ways to read cards, so you're going to practice these three main ways in order to learn what type of card reader you are. Also, the type of reader you are can shift and change as you practice, so I don't want you to think of this as a fixed truth.

1. Visual/Spiritual

For each of the cards, connect the images to your emotions. What do you feel when you look at this card? Forget, momentarily, what you know about the meaning of the cards or the words printed on them. Stay grounded in emotion/feelings, and what the image encourages you to feel, and not in ideas or language. Emotions are the language of Spirit, so you are most likely to make a connection and receive a message here, in this space.

A.) What did you feel while looking at the image on Card 1?

_____

_____

_____

B.) What did you feel while looking at the image on Card 2?

_____

_____

_____

After each reading, I want you to do a self-assessment to gauge your comfort level and success with this process.

C.) On a scale of **1 to 10**, with **10** being *"I was overcome with emotion and nearly brought to tears"* and **1** being *"I must be Vulcan,"* how emotional did you feel looking at the image on **Card 1**?

1   2   3   4   5   6   7   8   9   10

D.) On a scale of **1 to 10**, with **10** being *"I was overcome with emotion and nearly brought to tears"* and **1** being *"I must be Vulcan,"* how emotional did you feel looking at the image on **Card 2**?

1   2   3   4   5   6   7   8   9   10

E.) On a scale of **1 to 10**, with **10** being *"I felt God/Goddess/Universe speaking directly to me through the card"* and **1** being *"This is only cardboard,"* how much of a spiritual connection did you feel gazing at the image on **Card 1**?

1   2   3   4   5   6   7   8   9   10

F.) On a scale of **1 to 10**, with **10** being *"I felt God/Goddess/Universe speaking directly to me through the card"* and **1** being *"This is only cardboard,"* how much of a spiritual connection did you feel gazing at the image on **Card 2**?

1   2   3   4   5   6   7   8   9   10

2. Language

Now you're going to focus on language in your response to the cards. You can examine what the language printed on the cards means outside of a tarot/oracle context, or you can focus on the language that is commonly associated with that card (this exercise will look vastly different depending on if you have experience with tarot or not).

A.) What are all the word/language associations you have with **Card 1**?

_____

_____

B.) What are all the word/language associations you have with **Card 2**?

_____

_____

I'd like you to build upon your existing knowledge of this language. Now, we are going to narrow the scope and shift away from every word association we might have, and instead focus on tarot/oracle interpretations. Get out the book that came with your deck, and pull out at least two more resources. These can be other books you have on hand, or websites. Research each of your cards and compare/contrast information between sources.

C.) What new language can you identify for **Card 1**?

_____

_____

D.) What new language can you identify for **Card 2**?

_____

_____

Next, let's make a comparison of all your language associations to your emotional response.

E.) When you compare your language associations to your emotional response for **Card 1**, how well do they align, if at all?

_____

_____

F.) When you compare your language associations to your emotional response for **Card 2**, how well do they align, if at all?

_____

_____

G.) On a scale of **1 to 10** with **10** being, "*My emotional response and language associations were completely in alignment*" to "*Neither card seemed to connect my emotional response to its intended meaning,*" how well do you feel your spiritual and intellectual response to these two cards aligned?

1   2   3   4   5   6   7   8   9   10

Dream Journal

Use these pages to record all details from your dreams to use with the Dreams spreads.

"Ask, and it shall be given you: seek, and you will find; knock, and it shall be opened unto you"
-MATTHEW 7:7

Date: _____

_____

_____

_____

_____

_____

_____

_____

_____

_____

_____

_____

_____

_____

_____

_____

_____

_____

_____

_____

_____

_____

_____

_____

_____

Date: _____

Symbols	People

Events and Actions	Emotions

"Ask, and it shall be given you: seek, and you will find; knock, and it shall be opened unto you"
-MATTHEW 7:7

Date: _____

_____

_____

_____

_____

_____

_____

_____

_____

_____

_____

_____

_____

_____

_____

_____

_____

_____

_____

_____

_____

_____

_____

_____

_____

Date: _____

Symbols	People

Events and Actions	Emotions

Date: _____

_____
_____
_____
_____
_____
_____
_____
_____
_____
_____
_____
_____
_____
_____
_____
_____
_____
_____
_____
_____
_____
_____
_____
_____
_____
_____
_____
_____

Date: _____

Symbols	People

Events and Actions	Emotions

"Ask, and it shall be given you: seek, and you will find; knock, and it shall be opened unto you"
-Matthew 7:7

Date: _____

_____
_____
_____
_____
_____
_____
_____
_____
_____
_____
_____
_____
_____
_____
_____
_____
_____
_____
_____
_____
_____
_____
_____
_____
_____
_____
_____
_____

Date: _____

Symbols	People

Events and Actions	Emotions

"Ask, and it shall be given you: seek, and you will find; knock, and it shall be opened unto you"
-MATTHEW 7:7

Date: _____

_____

_____

_____

_____

_____

_____

_____

_____

_____

_____

_____

_____

_____

_____

_____

_____

_____

_____

_____

_____

_____

_____

_____

_____

_____

Date: _____

Symbols	People
Events and Actions	**Emotions**

"Ask, and it shall be given you: seek, and you will find; knock, and it shall be opened unto you"
-MATTHEW 7:7

Date: _____

_____
_____
_____
_____
_____
_____
_____
_____
_____
_____
_____
_____
_____
_____
_____
_____
_____
_____
_____
_____
_____
_____
_____
_____
_____
_____
_____
_____

Date: _____

Symbols	People

Events and Actions	Emotions

"Ask, and it shall be given you: seek, and you will find; knock, and it shall be opened unto you"
-MATTHEW 7:7

Date: _____

_____
_____
_____
_____
_____
_____
_____
_____
_____
_____
_____
_____
_____
_____
_____
_____
_____
_____
_____
_____
_____
_____
_____
_____
_____
_____
_____
_____
_____

Date: _____

Symbols	People

Events and Actions	Emotions

"Ask, and it shall be given you: seek, and you will find; knock, and it shall be opened unto you"
-MATTHEW 7:7

Date: _____

_____

_____

_____

_____

_____

_____

_____

_____

_____

_____

_____

_____

_____

_____

_____

_____

_____

_____

_____

_____

_____

_____

*" The personal life deeply lived always expands into truths beyond itself. " – **ANAÏS NIN***

Date: _____

Symbols	People

Events and Actions	Emotions

"Ask, and it shall be given you: seek, and you will find; knock, and it shall be opened unto you"
-MATTHEW 7:7

Date: _____

_____

_____

_____

_____

_____

_____

_____

_____

_____

_____

_____

_____

_____

_____

_____

_____

_____

_____

_____

_____

_____

_____

_____

_____

Date: _____

Symbols	People

Events and Actions	Emotions

"Ask, and it shall be given you: seek, and you will find; knock, and it shall be opened unto you"
-MATTHEW 7:7

Date: _____

_____

_____

_____

_____

_____

_____

_____

_____

_____

_____

_____

_____

_____

_____

_____

_____

_____

_____

_____

_____

_____

_____

_____

Date: _____

Symbols	People

Events and Actions	Emotions

"Ask, and it shall be given you: seek, and you will find; knock, and it shall be opened unto you"
-MATTHEW 7:7

Date: _____

_____

_____

_____

_____

_____

_____

_____

_____

_____

_____

_____

_____

_____

_____

_____

_____

_____

_____

_____

_____

_____

_____

_____

_____

" The personal life deeply lived always expands into truths beyond itself. " – **ANAÏS NIN**

Date: _____

Symbols	People
Events and Actions	**Emotions**